LUCK IS NOT A STRATEGY

An Executive Guidebook for Leading Change Initiatives

Janet Ply, PhD

Pendére Press

Luck is Not a Strategy/ Janet Ply. -- 1st ed. Pendére Press
ISBN 978-1-7368778-0-7

To Tammi

Contents

Contents (continued)

INTRODUCTION

"Be not afraid of growing slowly, be afraid only of standing still." ~ Chinese Proverb

Changing an organization to align it with your strategy is arguably one of the most difficult endeavors you'll undertake.

It's why there have been thousands of books written about leading change, managing transformations, leadership, project management, and related business topics. Many of these books are helpful, others not so much. Some are heavy on nuts and bolts and overhauling industries. Others offer pie-in-the-sky theories.

This book has a single purpose:

To provide executive practitioners a perspective on how to position change initiatives to improve the chances of success.

These are important and complex topics because they weave together art (humans) and science (process and strategy); my work has literally made a science of studying what makes endeavors successful and what makes them fail.

Over the past 25 years, I've documented and lived the good, the bad, and the ugly. I've seen the inner workings of industry from different angles as a consultant, client, vendor, or integrator. I've interviewed numerous C-Suite executives to learn what he or she would have done differently, as well as what they did well while managing transformation change efforts. In addition, I've read hundreds of related books and articles over the years to continue learning what others in this field shared.

A common finding is many executives underestimate the complexity of transformation change efforts. To understand this more, let's distinguish the difference between complex and complicated:

- *Complicated* is understood to mean large numbers.
- *Complex* means interdependence and connections.

As an example, implementing a change among 1,000 plumbers might be complicated, but probably not complex, as there is little-to-no communication and interdependence among them. On the other hand, trying to implement changes across two departments, such as sales and production, is complex because they are directly connected and may have conflicting goals, even though there are only two entities involved.

If we doubled the number of plumbers, would it be twice as difficult to implement the change? No, it would likely add more time.

However, if we add two more interdependent departments, there are exponentially more connections. Now we are dealing with four internal entities, and the complexity is much more than double.

THE PROBLEM EXECUTIVES OFTEN MISS

When teams have been successful executing on programs or projects, their efforts were most likely *linear* rather than *exponential* efforts. These linear successes led teams to a false conclusion—believing what is needed is more of the same and everything should be fine.

Here's the problem with following this line of thought. We're not factoring in the complexity of the changes. The exponential complexity factor associated with enterprise-level undertakings contributes to the demise of over two-thirds of enterprise initiatives which fail to deliver the expected business value or are scrapped entirely.

For those of you who have succeeded (and failed) in implementing enterprise change initiatives or other large-scale, complex programs, you have first-hand knowledge of exponential complexity and the impact of not taking into consideration aligning, planning, executing, and monitoring the activity.

From my collection of experiences and research, I've learned what's required for executives who are leading transformational efforts to be successful. And, spoiler alert, it's not luck. The topics included in this book have been curated for the level of understanding an executive team needs.

This book is not intended to make the executive team experts, rather to provide awareness and an appropriate level of detail ensuring areas are not overlooked.

For example, the sponsor needs to know current and future state business process mapping may need to be included as a project, but they don't need to know how to map the processes. Or they may need to be aware of possible roles of a Program Management Office (PMO) but don't need to know how to build one or create project schedules.

As you read this book, I suggest you view it as a guidebook for yourself and your teams. It creates a common framework and language you can share to stay connected and aligned, even as you delegate responsibilities to your teams.

Reflection questions are included at the end of most chapters of this book as a reminder of the key elements to consider. A summary of the reflection questions is provided in the Appendix as a checklist for positioning the initiative for success.

READINESS—YOU, YOUR TEAM, AND ORGANIZATION

"Leadership is the ability to translate a vision into reality." ~ Warren Bennis

CHAPTER 1

ORGANIZATIONAL CHANGE MANAGEMENT

Let's start by defining what is meant by organizational change management. There are several definitions in the literature. The one I like best is:

> *Managing the change that occurs when an organization undertakes work that spans the enterprise, or at a minimum, impacts several cross-functional areas.*

Change initiatives are usually transformational in nature, meaning they are designed to create a shift in the culture and to produce significant performance improvements. As such, there are likely massive changes to processes, people, and technology.

Examples of change initiatives include:

- New system implementations and business processes
- Consolidations or reorganizations
- Mergers or acquisitions

- Process improvement initiatives
- Outsourcing multiple functions.
- Acquisitions by equity firms with high expectations.

The problem begins when the complexity and resistance to change are almost always underestimated. The need to deal with and manage the people part of transforming an organization can be every bit as time consuming and critical as the strategic and tactical planning associated with the items listed above.

MY WAY OR THE HIGHWAY

On more than one occasion, I've heard executives say they will dictate the changes, and people can either get on board or leave. If it were only that simple! If only you could send an email, tweet, text, or TikTok, and then watch as everything and everyone magically falls into place. But you must remember whether we like it or not, we're dealing with human beings, and humans are messy, emotional, and irrational, even on good days. Taking an if-you're-hungry-you'll-eat-it approach will result in zero commitment to the change, and what a colleague calls *passive disobedience*. This is where people nod their heads yes and act in a perfunctory way, and then quietly look for ways to sink your plan.

A senior executive lamenting in hindsight about a transformation initiative to substantially reduce headcount provided this observation, *"We should've used a scalpel, and instead we used a baseball bat."*

For those employees who remained at the organization, employee engagement and morale were low, and many of the top performers left for positions with other companies.

With the never-ending challenge of finding and retaining highly skilled people, organizational change management is more important than ever.

SELECT A CHANGE MANAGEMENT MODEL

Since you've decided against the my-way-or-the-highway approach (you did make this decision, right?), you need to select a change management model to help guide the human aspects of the initiative.

If you use a consulting firm to help, you'll find many have their own preferred approaches for leading change.

If you've decided to go it alone, there are numerous commercially available models to pick from.

The key takeaway is to follow a proven-to-work change management methodology you believe fits you, your team, and your organization. The only wrong answer is NOT picking a model to follow.

Reflection Questions:

1. Do I have a good understanding of the magnitude of the impact of the change initiative?
2. Have I selected a change management approach for leading the change aspects of the initiative?

CHAPTER 2

ORGANIZATIONAL CHANGE READINESS

The difference between a successful undertaking and a failed one may very well come down to how well you really understand the impacts of the change initiative under consideration. As well as how much stress the organization is currently under.

Formulating the answers to the questions below will inform your thinking and allow your biases to be put aside. These are simple questions to ask. They take time to answer and require you to ask and listen carefully. Ask yourself the following four questions to better understand the magnitude of the change initiative:

1. **What is the scope of the change** (how many groups or departments are affected)?
2. **How many employees will be impacted** (new ways of working, new tools, different skills, reduced staff)?
3. **What are the types of changes**

4. What is the delta in change from where we are today versus where we expect to be once the change initiative is complete?

Doing a comprehensive review of the answers to these questions will help drive the strategy for planning out the change initiative.

UNDERSTAND THE CHARACTERISTICS OF THE ORGANIZATION

The second part of organizational change readiness is understanding the characteristics of the organization. This is done by assessing areas such as:

- The amount of change currently underway
- Leadership capabilities
- Company culture and values
- Results of prior change initiatives
- Employee readiness for change.

Below are questions for consideration when thinking about how ready your organization is for change:

1. **What other initiatives or situations are underway in your organization and causing organizational stress?** For example, to keep up with expectations are team members already working long hours? Have there been recent layoffs impacting morale? Or does a major pandemic have many of your people working from home and already stressed to their limits?

2. **What is the culture of the organization or affected groups?** Some organization leaders expect constant change, while others may have the attitude, *we've always done it this way*. The latter example is usually reflective of industries where employees have decades

of tenure and are resistant to change. Change will sometimes only happen when it is necessary for survival, but by then, it may be too late.

3. **What experience does your organization's leaders have in leading initiatives requiring significant organizational change?** What is the level of trust in the leadership team? What is the managerial style of the leaders? Are they experienced, willing to participate, and supportive? Or will they hope things go well and place blame when they don't?

4. **How well has the organization delivered on prior initiatives of this nature?** On average, 70 percent of large programs fail. Is the leadership team credible in their ability to deliver?

5. **What is the scope of the changes resulting from the initiative?** How might departments, roles, and employees be impacted? What types of change are expected in terms of automation, technology, business processes, mergers, outsourcing, or a combination of some or all of these?

6. **Will the affected groups be willing to support the changes needed?** What has been the track record in the past? How aware are the teams of the needed changes?

7. **How much effort will be required for operational readiness in terms of training, business process changes, policy and procedure changes, and new technology?** What knowledge or skill gaps exist?

The organizational readiness information is used to support change management planning, such as: selecting an executive sponsor; structuring the leadership team; selecting a change management team; uncovering risks, issues, and obstacles requiring attention; selecting a change management model; defining communication and training needs; and planning for the overall change management strategy.

UNDERSTAND THE EMPLOYEE PERCEPTION OF CHANGE

Organizational change readiness assessments include data collection from employees about their perception of the changes, how they will be impacted, and their perception of the organization's ability to implement change.

An employee statement rating their own change perception might be similar to these examples:

- The change supports my career aspirations.
- I am confident I have or can learn new skills to perform well in my new role.
- My job is not at risk as a result of the changes expected.

Statements from the employee in regard to their perception of organizational change might include:

- My organization has successfully implemented changes in the past.
- The organization takes care of employees who are adversely affected by the changes.
- Executives are experienced change leaders and sponsors of change.
- The organization is receptive to feedback and alternate ideas.

If you don't have in-house expertise to conduct an in-depth change readiness assessment, consider leveraging companies with this expertise. Sometimes the result of a change readiness assessment shows the level of change occurring in the organization to be counterproductive and introducing a significant change management initiative is likely doomed before it starts . Even under the worst circumstances, an expert can help you determine options after reviewing a properly conducted readiness assessment.

Reflection Questions:

1. Do I have a good understanding of the scope of the initiative?
2. Should an organizational readiness assessment be conducted?

CHAPTER 3

KNOWING WHY AND COMMUNICATING THE VISION

Implementing change because I said so sometimes works on your kids, but almost never with your employees. Simon Sinek's YouTube video on the *Golden Circle of Moving from the Inside Out–Why, How, What* applies to change as well. Inspiring leaders start with the why, not the what. People buy into why you do something, not what you do.

Imagine standing in front of your employees, telling them you're going to bring in a consulting firm to redo business processes and change systems so you'll be more competitive. What do you think their reaction will be?

How different would the message be if you were to remind everyone of the successes and good events happening because of your company's products or services? Explain further how, to be able to do even better, changes need to be made?

> *Bonus tip: If you don't have someone on your team who can be an objective sounding board for communication before it goes live, that's a critical gap to fill.*

FINDING YOUR WHY

Why do you believe the change is necessary? Albert Einstein said, *"If I had an hour to solve a problem, I'd spend 55 minutes thinking about the problem and five minutes thinking about solutions."* He believed the quality of the solution you develop is proportional to the ability to identy the problem you want to solve. Understanding the problem makes it easier to define the why.

We, humans, are motivated by the why. We act because we agree with the why. The vision for the change initiative must provide direction, create alignment across the organization, and connect to the organization's mission and vision.

Change initiatives introduce uncertainty, fear, and anxiety in the workplace, requiring us to move out of our comfort zone. Most people like their comfort zone and are quite happy with their routines. Fear of the unknown and uncertainty causes physical and emotional reactions that create resistance to change.

Employee resistance to change is a key factor in the failure of many transformation initiatives. Leaders need to listen (really listen) to the employees to understand these concerns and fears so they can be addressed as part of the vision.

Executives leading change cannot assume the employees understand the reasoning behind why changes are needed and what we risk by not changing. What you see and what they see may be quite different. Sometimes changes are needed to enable a company to grow (or maybe, survive).

A software development company needed the cash infusion afforded by an equity partner to remain viable in the marketplace and to accelerate product development. The equity partner bought a majority share and, in return, expected the company to make changes in how it was structured and managed. This, of course, was met with much resistance from the leadership team and employees. Once the CEO explained this move was necessary for long-term viability and to continue adding value to the client base, the resistance gradually started to fade.

You want and need employee buy-in. It is essential to invest the time to understand the why and communicate it to all the stakeholders. Good leaders develop the story that clearly outlines why the change is needed, how it aligns with the organization's vision, and the positive outcomes in the future.

FACT-BASED STORIES VS. FEAR-BASED STORIES

Rest assured, if you, as the leader, don't write and communicate the story, employees will write their own version that will likely be quite different. Even when you believe you've done a good job of explaining the why, there will still be resistance. Fearful employees will create stories to legitimize their desire to stay in the comfort zone, and these stories will spread and become significant inhibitors.

I learned this first-hand when working for a large data management company which was functioning like a start-up, even though it had been in business for decades. By start-up, I mean there were few processes and tools in place. There was no portfolio management. The average schedule overrun on a six-month project was another six months, roles and responsibilities were vague, and there was little accountability. I know, sounds perfect, right?

My role was to build an enterprise PMO: put people, processes, and tools in place, and improve the organizational process maturity for the delivery organization within the company. After hiring experienced project managers, developing the project management methodology for the company to follow, and providing project management training, we were ready to implement an enterprise project management tool for capturing and managing project work, resources, and time tracking.

This initiative had executive sponsorship at the C-suite. There had been extensive communications through town halls, emails, newsletters, and department meetings on why a project management platform was necessary.

The change made perfect sense to the leadership team as to why this was needed:

- The delivery organization was losing money because of late and inconsistent project delivery.
- Credibility had been lost with several long-standing clients who were moving their work to competitors.
- To survive as a company, leadership must improve project delivery capabilities. Good progress had been made improving skills in project management. To continue building in this area, a solution was needed to better initiate and manage projects. It was understood training and mentoring would be provided to ensure success and make the needed changes to work habits.

The purpose of our enterprise project management solution included the following:

- Ability to understand resource constraints and better manage workloads.
- Improve project estimation accuracy by building a historical estimation database.
- Improve profitability by having more realistic estimates for fixed price projects.
- Increase credibility with clients by doing what was promised in the timeframe promised.
- By having the work outlined in a project schedule, we would:
  - Do a more thorough job of capturing all the work required to complete the project.
  - Improve ability to negotiate price and schedule with clients.
  - Receive buy-in from team members to complete their work on time, building a culture of accountability, trust, and reliability.
- Improve visibility into schedule and budget to see what progress has been made and how much it has cost.
- Identify problems sooner when they are easier to correct.
- Create dashboards to provide insights into project performance for executives.

While all this makes perfect sense to mature organizations, below are stories, takeaways, and questions from some of the managers and employees:

- We are implementing a Slacker Tracker.
- Tracking the number of hours I work takes away valuable time I could spend working on my project.

- Time spent on planning projects is time I can spend doing project work.
- Why should I spend time planning when I know what I'm doing?
- Report 40 hours a week, regardless of the time worked so no one knows if you worked more or less than full time.
- Will I be fired if the amount of time I work on my tasks is greater than the amount of time I estimated?
- Even if someone is working part-time, I'm going to tell them to report full-time hours so they aren't reassigned.
- If I'm not assigned to a project, will I be fired?
- What will happen to me if my project is late and it's not my fault?
- What if the project management software is too complicated and I can't learn it or use it effectively?

While we thought we had done a good job communicating the why for this solution, it became clear we didn't adequately address employee or supervisor concerns and questions. Implementation of the solution was not the time to have an angry or an emotional *because I said so* reaction.

This miss on the part of the leadership team had to be corrected before we could move forward.

Ultimately, the solution was successfully implemented. It took time, training, mentoring, and patience to remove the fear and anxieties of the employees.

No matter what your timeline is, the lesson will likely take longer because you cannot rush the process of employee adoption. Fred Brooks in *The Mythical Man-Month* says, *"You can't take nine women and make a baby in one month."*

There will be a gestation period for employee adoption. How long the gestation is depends on how well the leadership team does their job.

THE HUMAN ASPECTS OF CHANGE MANAGEMENT

Managing the human aspects of change requires the precision of a scalpel.

More times than not, executives stand in front of employees at town halls and say, "We need to change," and explain the rationale from the organizational perspective, neglecting the employees' perspectives and what's in it for them.

As a result, many employees have blank stares and start surfing through LinkedIn and Indeed. And, they may have a legitimate reason to be concerned. Some skills being used today are not the skills needed in the future. Employees may fear learning new skills will be too challenging, and they will fail in new jobs. Productivity starts to drop as water-cooler and instant messaging chatter increases, causing fear to start permeating throughout the organization and productivity to nosedive.

KEY POINTS TO KEEP IN MIND WHEN CONSIDERING THE HUMAN ASPECT

Keep people informed. In times of uncertainty, we need MORE communication, not less. Lack of communication begets uncertainty, and uncertainty, in turn, begets insecurity. Even if there is nothing new to report, connect on a regular basis.

Listen. It's not uncommon for directors and senior managers to simply communicate the same messages handed down to them by executives, but no one really knew what would be asked of them and how the changes would affect them. Directors and senior managers who realize how essential communication is at all levels of the organization will listen, engage in conversations, understand concerns, and tailor the information for the people receiving it.

Don't sugarcoat the message. As Bréne Brown says in her book, ***Dare to Lead***, *"Clear is kind; unclear is unkind."* Not communicating clearly to employees is unkind. When we think we know what's best for others, we are letting our egos stand in the way, assuming they are incapable of making their own decisions.

Minimize Attrition Risks. If there are concerns your key people may leave, bring them into the conversation early. Show them what the future looks like. Be honest about the work in front of them. Offer retention bonuses to keep them. Listen to their concerns and be patient as they work through the change curve because you are likely ahead of them.

Communicate. Communicate. Communicate. Most executives who have managed large transformation initiatives will say it's impossible to over-communicate. The trap that often occurs is if you're living the transformation every day, you forget others aren't, and they aren't as informed as you. If you are too far in front of your employees, you're not leading—you're out for a stroll. Having at least one skilled communications person who focuses on communicating with all the affected parties and who helps you develop your communication consciousness will be worth every penny.

Key point—this is about effective communication, not PR. On one large, high-profile program ($600M+), four full-time communications people were assigned. Their job was communicating program information internally, and to over

200 stakeholders, legislators, and other government entities. The best way to avoid rumors and unnecessary anxiety is consistent messaging and communications.

Cascading messages. Being able to communicate goals and the associated strategies to achieve those goals to an executive team is quite different from communicating what the vision and strategies mean to employees deeper in the organization.

Being able to cascade the appropriate messaging throughout an organization from top to bottom is a non-trivial task. This starts with understanding what is needed to implement the vision, from top to bottom. Let's take an example. During the annual planning session of a client organization, an overall goal was to increase the number of products sold by 50 percent while reducing the number of calendar days to produce each widget by 25 percent. This all sounds well and good, but what must happen to accomplish this? How does it translate to managers and individual contributors?

In this case, it meant the implementation of a system that could report how long it took a person to complete his or her part at each step of the production process. It meant changes to the processes and how tasks had been completed in the past, an increase in outsourcing, and implementing accountability which not been in place before. Performance became the basis for pay increases and promotions.

Know your stakeholders. Changes to how work has been finished in the past will likely affect your stakeholders. Clients tend not to like surprises and need to be kept informed of what they should expect. Vendors may need to make changes to systems or provide additional services. Outsourcing vendors need to know how changes affect the services they provide.

Be aware of any stakeholder who is affected by the change initiative.

Adoption and Stickability. Embracing and adopting change to ensure long-term stickability is hard. Our brains are wired to be uncomfortable with change. Doing things in a different way takes us out of our comfort zone. One way to encourage the adoption of new ways of taking action is to tie it into a person's or team's compensation, recognition, or some other incentive of value to a person.

A large financial services company was implementing a process improvement initiative that significantly changed the way over 2,000 software developers did their jobs. The initiative was properly staffed with some of the best people in the world leading it, and we had a sufficient budget. A team of highly trained organization change management folks kept everyone informed of what was coming, how the work was changing, the required training, and the expected benefits.

The teams' technology workload was reduced. This provided them the time to take the classes and restructure their projects in accordance with the new way of working. Still, the teams were slow to engage.

The president of the company sent out an email informing the teams he was going to give the highly coveted Presidential Award to the first five teams to be assessed at the desired level of compliance. This award was $5,000 to each employee on the team and a leaded-glass pyramid signifying a high achievement within the company.

Within hours of the announcement, project managers started calling, asking to schedule an assessment. Teams worked nights and weekends to be eligible to receive this award. While the payout totaled over $100,000, it was still far less expensive than the amount of money it would have cost the company to continue its current track. Morale was high and employees were engaged.

Using incentives, such as compensation, recognition, or competition, as the scalpel over the bat is a better choice every time. Use the appropriate reward system to resonate with each person or profession.

Reflection Questions

1. Have I aligned compensation, recognition, and reinforcement to support the organizational change?
2. What steps have I taken to put individual and team goals, at all levels, in sync with the company goals?
3. Is the vision communicated in terms that are appropriate to all levels within the company?

CHAPTER 4

EXECUTIVE SPONSORSHIP

Welcome to the section of this book that's all about you! If you were to line up all the failed strategic transformation initiatives across organizations and look at the root causes of failure, the absence of executive sponsorship (or choosing the wrong person for this role) would be at the top of the list.

An engaged sponsor with resources and a vested interest in the initiative will likely be the difference between a successful initiative and a failed one.

If you aren't the executive sponsor, you must carefully consider who you will select. This is not something you can simply delegate or internally outsource. When everyone knows it matters to you, it will begin to matter to them. Who you name to be the sponsor and how you set them up for success will speak volumes to the truth.

Transformation initiatives are cross-functional in nature. They require sponsorship by senior members of the leadership team, very often from the C-suite.

Ideally, the person who can make decisions across the functional areas is the optimal sponsor. However, this may be the CEO or someone in the C-suite who doesn't have the time to provide this level of oversight.

What do you do if that's the case?

We'll consider that in a moment, but first, be clear about the characteristics you are looking for in an effective sponsor.

TRAITS OF AN EFFECTIVE SPONSOR

The success of a change initiative hinges on the person at helm. The executive sponsor models servant leadership, helping the teams achieve their goals by being actively involved.

One day during the American Revolutionary War, Washington rode up to a group of soldiers trying to raise a beam to a high position. The corporal overseeing the work kept shouting words of encouragement, but they couldn't manage to do it.

After watching their lack of success, Washington asked the corporate why he didn't join in and help.

The corporal replied quickly, "Do you realize that I'm the corporal?"

Washington politely replied, "I beg your pardon, Mr. Corporal, I did."

Washington dismounted his horse and went to work with the soldiers until the beam was in place. Wiping perspiration from his face, he said, "If you should need help again, call on Washington, your commander-in-chief, and I will come." (John Maxwell, *Five Levels of Leadership*)

A successful executive sponsor has a servant leader mindset and is willing to step in and help as needed. Other traits to consider when selecting the executive sponsor include:

- Has led transformations of this magnitude and complexity in the past.
- Has the ability to provide a clear definition of the overall goals and objectives for the initiative and set the overall scope.
- Clearly articulates the business case and rationale for why the initiative is needed at his or her level.
- Understands and communicates clearly to all affected groups how the changes associated with the initiative are aligned to the overall corporate strategy.
- Understands and communicates the impact of the changes to each affected group and, specifically, what must change.
- Has strong communication skills for credibility, to encourage feedback, and to provide clear messaging.
- Is strongly motivated and committed to making the needed changes.
- Has prioritized the portfolio of projects and resources to reflect the importance of the change.
- Has good working relationships throughout the organization and is well respected.
- Has a history of successfully leading change initiatives and understands the associated complexities.
- Has committed to providing the resources needed to achieve the objectives of the changes.
- Has tied the desired behaviors into employee performance management.

- Has mechanisms in place for planning, tracking progress, and managing scope, budget, risks, issues across the initiative, and re-planning.
- Has the ability or credibility to manage competing stakeholder interests and negotiate a common solution everyone can support.
- Walks with confidence on top of water.

So, the last bullet isn't really a pre-requisite, but the list may feel a bit overwhelming. However, it underscores the importance of the decision you will make when selecting the executive sponsor if it's not you.

Being the executive sponsor of a large change initiative requires a lot of time and focus and is not an addition to someone's day job.

Why? Because the sponsor needs to be available to the program managers, functional teams, and stakeholder groups to set direction, ensure the right resources are provided, and resolve issues. The executive sponsor manages competing stakeholder interests and negotiates solutions those affected can support. It is almost always a full-time job.

Simply adding the sponsorship role of a large transformation initiative to the executive sponsor's workload is almost sure to cause the initiative to fail.

It may be worth considering backfilling the executive sponsor or reassigning some of his or her duties to free up the time needed to focus on the program. Be sensitive to the concern the executive sponsor may have if you remove his or her responsibilities except for the transformation initiative. To them, it may feel like a career-limiting move or very binary. They may try to convince you to allow them to keep their current responsibilities. To their way of thinking, this gives them a fallback plan.

Key reflection question spoiler alert—if the transformation initiative fails, will you fire the executive sponsor or retain them?

CHOOSE WISELY

In addition to the traits above, the executive sponsor should be selected based on the type of transformation. Experience shows while most transformation initiatives include large system implementations, technology is an enabler for the business, not the primary owner. Avoid the temptation to make the Chief Information Officer (CIO) or Chief Technical Officer (CTO) the executive sponsor. He or she should be a member of the Executive Steering Committee but probably not the overall person in charge. You are transforming your entire business, not just the tech stack.

The Chief Operating Officer (COO) in an energy company refused to be the executive sponsor, citing "programs of this magnitude" were career-limiting. (We've seen some truth to that, especially where senior executives are named as Strategic Advisor to the Chief Executive Officer (CEO) during an organization reshuffle. Most everyone knows this new assignment is simply a step closer to the door for the leader and a way for everyone to save face.) Instead, the CIO was assigned as the executive sponsor, in addition to his day job, resulting in a no-win situation complete with program delays and failed project headlines in the major newspapers around the country. This wasn't the only cause of the program failure but it's where the problems began.

For career damage control, it's not uncommon to hear executives say they are bringing in a large consulting company to lead the effort. Their motivation is often to ensure there is an external company to blame when the initiative heads south. They know the likelihood of success is small and use phrases like this, "You won't get fired for bringing in (IBM), (Accenture), (big consulting firm)." Even using this approach requires strong executive sponsorship and oversight.

Keep in mind consultant-led change never sticks. Why? Because they don't have to live with whatever the aftermath is. They don't understand the culture. And, they simply don't have as much at stake as you do. So, be sure you are leveraging consulting firms appropriately and you embrace the responsibility that can't be outsourced.

Reflection Questions

1. Do I have someone on staff who has the characteristics to be an effective executive sponsor (if it's not me)? If not, how will I find and incentivize the person?

2. Are you prepared to provide constant and visible support to this person to increase the odds of success?

3. Is the executive sponsor taking on a pass or fail assignment? Why or why not?

4. If using a consulting company, do you have a clear understanding of what work should be completed by them and what you are be responsible for?

CHAPTER 5

ORGANIZATIONAL ALIGNMENT

Making sure everyone is on the same page (goals, approach) is challenging but necessary for the program to be successful. In a study by Clear Company, 97 percent of employees and executives believe lack of alignment within a team impacts the outcome of a project, and 86 percent cite lack of collaboration or ineffective communication for workplace failures.

Ron Carucci, in a Harvard Business Review article (How Leaders Get in the Way of Organizational Change, April 30, 2021), writes about his conversation with the Chief Transformation Officer in a midsize financial services company. *"We thought we'd done everything we needed to do to keep this transformation from derailing. We communicated relentlessly, held virtual town halls to engage people, and resourced dozens of initiatives to support the vision for change. But we've ended up with nothing but hamsters running on wheels. We've made no measurable progress, cynicism is setting in as people are mired in activities that feel futile, and we've long lost sight of the vision for why we started this journey in the first place."*

That statement is a good summary of how most leaders feel about their change initiatives.

When the organization is aligned, the work is well orchestrated and is performed more easily, faster, and with better results. Resources (human and otherwise) are available when needed, and they are more engaged; silos are broken down, and there is collaboration across teams, resulting in better communications, ideas, and processes, and decisions can be made more quickly.

Below are areas to consider for organizational alignment:

Organizational Strategy. The leadership team understands and communicates how the change initiative aligns with and supports the overall strategies of the organization and why it is important.

Leadership. The leadership teams must be cohesive units with clarity of purpose and focus. They must speak with one voice and model the desired behaviors. Non-supportive or unaligned leaders of the change can sabotage the efforts of the entire team. Taking the time for leaders to align with the overall program makes a challenging undertaking a little less challenging.

Leadership Roles. Leaders have clarity and clear expectations around their roles in leading change.

Vision. Everyone on the team must understand both the vision for the change initiative and the performance expectations for their team.

Success Measures. The teams should know what success looks like and how it will be measured. Consider applying these measures to employees' compensation or other motivators.

Priorities. Senior leaders of the initiative ensure the top priorities for teams are front and center, ensuring alignment across the organization and the right work is being completed at the right time by the right people.

Rules of Engagement. The senior leadership team has responsibility for developing, communicating, and implementing the rules of engagement—in other words, how the initiative will be run. This includes topics like the overall program organization structure, a sense of urgency, expectations for working together, and processes to be followed.

Decision-making. Everyone needs to know who the decision-makers are and how decisions are made. Also, what decisions can be made at the team level and which ones require someone higher in the organization to make them?

Decision Stickiness. Once a decision is made, it's time to accept and focus on the work that needs to be performed. If the process for decision-making is clear, there should be few, if any, instances where a decision should be second-guessed.

Escalation. All team members should know when and how to escalate an issue. Waiting too long to bring an issue to a leader's attention may have long-term implications that could have been avoided.

Communicate. Communicate. Communicate. Good, frequent communication keeps everyone aligned with the goal and informed about the overall progress of the project. Communication is critical in every area. Even in this book you will see us drive this message forward multiple times.

Reflection Questions

1. Does the leadership team understand how the change initiative fits into the overall organizational strategy?
2. Does each leader have clarity around his or her role?
3. Do we have measurement and reporting in place to track the effectiveness of the project?
4. Is there clarity around who the decision-makers are and how decisions will be made?

CHAPTER 6

TALENT ASSESSMENT

For many companies, delivering on a highly complex, enterprise-wide, multiyear (yes, years, and not months) change initiative to significantly transform the organization is unchartered territory. Because these types of initiatives aren't commonplace, organizations often don't have the talent needed to lead.

People who have successfully led projects and programs of low complexity often fail when placed in leadership roles on enterprise-wide initiatives. A client executive was providing an overview of how a large program was failing miserably. This was a large, complex program that my client was responsible for delivering on behalf of one of their largest clients, a Fortune 50 company. I'll never forget one of his comments:

> *"This is the first time that we haven't been able to just grind our way through a project."*

Welcome to enterprise complexity, where grinding your way through seldom works, and where you can't scale brute force.

Enthusiasm is NOT Equal to Experience

It's not uncommon for someone in an organization to say they want to take on a particular role because it's a growth opportunity. This is not the time to put someone in an important role and hope they will figure it out. There is far too much at stake. If a person doesn't have the expertise or have someone who can provide mentorship, this is setting them—and you—up for failure. This is true of all key roles, from executive sponsor to project manager to team leads.

In Jim Collins' book, *Good to Great*, he writes about getting the right people on the bus. Staffing the leadership and subject matter expert roles with the right people for an enterprise initiative is a critical success factor.

Having the wrong people on the bus, especially in senior leadership roles, is almost a guarantee there will be significant problems, likely moving the change initiative into the bucket with the 70 percent of change initiatives which fail.

Think about the carnage left behind when you choose a weak or poor leader: key people leave the organization, morale is lower, and productivity drops. Take the time to put the right leaders in the right roles and provide them with the support they need.

Change initiatives require flexibility and willingness to pivot. Future-state processes are less clear and will likely evolve, tactics may need to be revised, and success may require as much art as science.

Leaders and other key team members need an open mindset. Being too rigid and dogmatic may force someone off the bus.

TEAM CHARACTERISTICS TO LOOK FOR INCLUDE:

- Flexibility and agility
- Open to new ways of thinking, working, and behaving
- Decision making (a bias towards action)
- Learners
- Motivation
- Deep business acumen
- Change agents
- Growth mindset
- Ability to lead
- Change management experience
- Experience with type of initiative being implemented.

Reflection Questions:

1. Have I performed an assessment of the leadership team to determine if each person has the right skills and experience to lead his or her area?
2. Do the leaders have the right attributes for leading a change initiative?
3. Do I have the right people on the bus?

ART—LEADING PEOPLE THROUGH CHANGE

"The secret of change is to focus all your energy not on fighting the old, but on building the new." ~Socrates

CHAPTER 7

LEADERSHIP

There are thousands of books written on the topic of leadership. How to be a good leader. Characteristics of good leaders. The impact of bad leaders. And more, of course.

In my experience, the ultimate success or failure of a change program rests squarely on the shoulders of the leadership team.

In Chapter 5 of *The New Economics for Industry, Government, Education*, Dr. W. Edwards Deming writes:

> *"Transformation in any organization will take place under a leader. It will not be spontaneous."*

The senior leadership team is responsible for recognizing the need for change. This team develops a clear vision, establishes desired outcomes for the change, and communicates the definition of success. They develop the tactics for implementing the change, set priorities, identify potential risks, and lay out the high-level game plan–after listening to questions and concerns throughout the organization.

SUCCESSFUL LEADERS COMMUNICATE

Leadership is about communicating the what behind the change and the why and the how. The leadership team is responsible for ensuring proper planning, staffing, and execution controls are in place—not taking the Ready, Fire, Aim approach. Take the time to position the initiative to be successful. Avoid the *Never enough time to do it right the first time, but always enough time to do it over and over and over* mindset. If you're going to position the initiative to be successful, the senior leadership team must have or acquire the leadership skills necessary to lead an organization through change. Focusing only on results is a recipe for failure.

RECIPE FOR SUCCESS

In successful change initiatives, effective leaders spend significant time engaging everyone involved in the change initiative, understanding change is hard for most people. Oftentimes, people are concerned they will lose their jobs, they won't be able to learn the new ways of working because of the change, or there could be a sense of loss. Good leaders emphasize the human aspects of change, including their own.

John Maxwell defines leadership this way:

"Leadership is influence—nothing more, nothing less."

This is key when leading change initiatives where the leadership team needs to influence possibly an entire organization to persuade the people this change is needed. To influence, leaders must have trust and credibility.

They take the time to explain why change is needed and how the employees will be supported throughout the change.

They invest the time early to get buy-in from the people who will be affected by the change because they know it will substantially reduce resistance and accelerate the work. Simply telling someone they need to change their practices and habits without understanding their fears and concerns is a recipe for disaster.

Leaders continue to receive feedback throughout the initiative by asking questions—they don't assume they have all the answers. Leaders listen and learn without judging the person who is providing the information.

Leaders are coaches, not judges. They help people understand what is needed and set clear expectations. As mentioned earlier, *clear is kind; unclear is unkind.*

Too often, weak leaders give orders and either think or hope the recipient of these orders can carry them out. We've all been in meetings where a senior person yells at their team and tells them to fix a problem. Seriously, do any of us think that's going to work and have sustained results? Don't you think they would fix it if they knew how?

Real leaders strive to understand the issues, the root causes, the range of solutions and trade-offs, and help come up with a decision and plan of action.

REFLECTION QUESTIONS:

1. Does the leadership team have leadership skills and experience to successfully lead the change initiative?
2. Do I understand the concerns and fears of the people who will be affected by the change and a plan in place to manage this?

CHAPTER 8

CHANGE IS HARD

W e all know change is hard. Kegan and Lahey summarize the challenge well in *Immunity to Change:*

> *"Not long ago, a medical study showed that if heart doctors tell their seriously at-risk heart patients they will literally die if they to not make changes to their personal lives—diet, exercise, smoking—still only one in seven is actually able to make the changes. One in seven! And we can safely assume that the other six wanted to live, see more sunsets, watch their grandchildren grow up. They didn't lack a sense of urgency. The incentives for change couldn't be greater. The doctors made sure they knew just what they needed to do. Still, they couldn't do it."*

Think about this—you are leading a change initiative that potentially affects hundreds or thousands of people and only one out of seven will change their behavior to save their lives! You need them to change the way they work, learn new skills, fit into new organizational structures—none of which is life-threatening! It's no wonder that the failure rate for change is so high.

Common Causes of Failures

As mentioned earlier, over 70 percent of change initiatives fail. We know what causes them to fail, and yet the same mistakes are made over and over and over.

In other industries, people see an issue and they create corrective or preventive actions to rectify or improve upon it for next time. Think about the number of recalls on cars and the expense automakers incur to correct problems. Leaders in manufacturing plants understand the importance of quality and correcting the root causes of defects. Yet, in our business of leading change initiatives, we see the same known issues over and over and still don't take corrective actions.

Common causes of large program failures are well documented, regardless of industry, company size, or type of change initiatives.

The root causes for failure almost always include a combination of some (or all) of the following with minor variations:

- Underestimating the resistance to change
- Lack of or wrong executive sponsor
- Weak or wrong people in key leadership roles
- Unrealistic expectations set upfront, especially unrealistic deadlines with no basis
- Unclear communications
- Unclear scope definition
- Too few or the wrong people on project teams
- Expecting people to work on the change initiative in addition to their day jobs

- Poorly written contracts with key vendors
- Lack of understanding of overall complexity of the initiative
- Skipping or poorly performing key steps along the way (e.g., business process mapping, requirements).

Basically, everything included in this book.

We know the right way to position a change initiative to be successful, and yet organizations continue to make the same mistakes.

We know the burner is hot. We've seen other people touch it. Maybe we've touched it before, but then we think, *Well, maybe it's not now?* Trust me, it is.

WHY WE DON'T LEARN

There are several reasons why we don't seem to learn from our mistakes. Culture is one of the biggest contributors to the success or failure of implementing change. Culture has been said to eat strategy for breakfast.

Consider where your organization's culture falls when it comes to change:

- Is your culture one of accountability, or one where the managers are laid back, and there are few consequences?
- Is the organization structure one where accountability cannot be established?
- Do employees trust the leadership team?
- Do you have an authoritarian culture where you monitor hours worked and how much time people are logged in and what they're doing?
- Do you have a *we've always done it this way* mindset?

- Do people work well together across departments, or do they want to stay in their own silos?
- Are people penalized when they make mistakes, or are they encouraged and rewarded for taking risks?
- Are rewards aligned with desired behaviors?

Careful review of your answers to these questions may reveal the likelihood you are basing decisions on inaccurate information.

An example of reward and desired behaviors being misaligned was uncovered in the software development group of one large telecom company. I learned senior managers and directors had been making up software development productivity numbers to receive their bonuses.

I couldn't figure out why these leaders were adamant against tracking time to measure team productivity.

There was pushback from people stating it violated labor laws and since no one had tracked time before, it couldn't possibly be implemented now—people would quit in droves and go to competitors where they weren't required to track their time.

After much probing and investigating, I learned bonuses were tied to the reported productivity that was fabricated each month.

I shared this finding with the CEO, and he promptly changed the bonus structure to align with time tracking and accurate productivity numbers.

Once the bonus structure changed, miraculously there were no longer any labor law violations with time tracking and it became a great idea!

ASK FOR HELP

As the executive reading this book, you don't have to go it alone, nor should you. There are thousands of other executives who have traveled this road and are willing to share their hard-won lessons. Ask questions about how they addressed and considered cultural challenges, incentives, communications—everything you can think of.

Engage a consulting company specializing in organizational change management and leading transformational intiatives if needed.

It's OK to stop and ask for directions.

Reflection Questions:

1. Who do I know and can speak with who has experience in leading change initiatives?
2. Am I, and is my leadership team, willing to listen and learn from others?
3. Successful change is contingent upon several key factors or drivers. Do I know the drivers of my change? If so, how will I locate other learners who faced the same or similar drivers?

CHAPTER 9

BUILDING TEAM RELATIONSHIPS AND NETWORKS

We've already established change initiatives are complex, and the great majority of them fail. Building strong and trusted relationships across teams will go a long way in eliminating much of the stress that comes with complex interactions, tight schedules, escalations, and unusual dynamics.

There will be plenty of opportunities for people or teams to blame others when projects don't go well, especially if your organization is already practiced in playing the blame game. As a leader, you want your teams to reach across the aisle to help when another team is behind—not think about ways to place blame for delays or issues.

RELATIONSHIPS TAKE TIME

Take the time to build strong relationships that lead to high-performing teams. Dysfunctional teams that lack trust, place blame, hide bad news, or lack accountability and attention to detail will derail the work, putting the change initiative back in the 70 percent failure bucket. With the dramatic increase in remote work, relationship building is more critical than ever.

Regular team-building exercises and communications tend to break down barriers and allow people to see the human side of each other—include employees, contractors, vendors, partners, and team members of consulting companies. This is especially true with the trend of more people working remotely.

Learning about the interests and lives outside of work of those you interact with builds meaningful relationships and grows a network of colleagues. Think about how much time can be saved and stress eliminated when leaders across the change initiative feel comfortable with their team and peers. Reaching across departments to ask for help or to share useful information, talking directly to another team or vendor is easaier when time is taken to get to know and understand others. This habit is invaluable and especially useful when what's needed is someone to simply go the extra mile.

Here are some concepts and practices to consider for building relationships across teams:

- Foster open and honest communications across teams. Communication is honest, even when the news isn't great. Admitting you don't have all the answers but are willing to find out builds credibility and makes you approachable.
- Build trust across the teams. Everyone must feel safe sharing information, even when it is not the best results.
- Come together proactively to solve problems; not place blame.

- Express appreciation to those who have gone above and beyond in doing their job, especially when the extra effort was to help another team. This provides endless benefits to the organization.
- Remove toxic personalities or people who are in over their heads. This point gets extra emphasis. When you see either situation, you must act quickly.

RELATIONSHIPS ARE AN INVESTMENT, NOT AN EXPENSE

Time and money spent on team building pays off many times over, plus makes a happier, healthier working environment.

One company I worked for sent about 50 of us (all new hires) to a dude ranch for a long weekend. We didn't know each other except for an occasional meeting or seeing each other in the hallways. It was quite the experience. We had friendly competitions for riding a mechanical bull, using beer bottles as targets for .22-pistol shooting, and herding cattle. I think we had about a 1:1 ratio of cowboy to employee to keep us safe and out of trouble.

At the end of the weekend, we were all laughing, talking, or sleeping on the bus ride back home. Our working relationship was forever changed for the better, and we still tell stories about each other 20 years later.

The company leadership knew building these types of relationships would forge lifelong friendships and significantly improve how we all worked together.

While not every company has a budget to send 50 people to a dude ranch, there are many team-building ideas to build trust and camaraderie, such as potlucks, virtual happy hours, and an inexhaustible list of ideas found on the internet.

Reflection Questions:

1. What are the characteristics of my team? Do these characteristics point to high performance or dysfunctionality?
2. Are team-building activities scheduled regularly, even if some members are remote or virtual?
3. How am I as a leader, along with my leadership team, intentionally building rapport with your teams?

SCIENCE—BUILDING A POWERFUL PROJECT PLAN

"A goal without a plan is just a wish."
~ Antoine de Saint-Exuper

CHAPTER 10

PORTFOLIO MANAGEMENT

U p until this point, the focus of this book has been on the art of leading people and the human aspects of change management. The remainder of the book focus is on the science, the tactical aspects of positioning the change initiative for success.

A good understanding of what work has already been planned across the organization and the needed resources. Understanding this information will enable you to more easily determine the impact on resources for the transformation initiative.

KEY POINTS

Sometimes there is an expectation the additional work required to support the changes can simply be absorbed into the individual's workload. This rarely works out with teams becoming overworked, burned out, and frustrated, resulting in poorly delivered projects not providing the expected return on investment or worse case, simply failing.

It's not uncommon to find an organization doesn't have a clear picture of the projects, and programs already planned or underway. Even less common is to find an organization where leaders understand all the work planned and underway aligned with resources and budgets. Work that should be performed as a cohesive unit and managed as a program across functional departments becomes siloed and splintered.

JOB #1

Understanding what constitutes a project or program is the first step in establishing the organizational workload.

Portfolio management ensures the correct projects are being worked on at the right time to deliver the highest value to the organization. The workload is balanced with the resources available. Introducing a large, transformative initiative requires substantial additional efforts across the organization. (You do have a functioning portfolio management process, don't you?)

The portfolio management process determines what work is required for business as usual, what work can be postponed or canceled, and what resources will be required to support change initiatives.

Balancing the portfolio of projects within an organization is no small feat under the best of circumstances. Deciding to embark on an enterprise-wide change initiative requires a hard look at the projects across the organization to determine what is feasible—this is no time to be optimistic. Hope, like luck, is not a strategy! You may find the needed resources are already committed to other priorities and not available to support the change initiative.

Ongoing management of the portfolio of work requires a strong governance team. The governing body is responsible for selecting, prioritizing, and controlling the organization's projects and programs to ensure the work is aligned with goals, and there are sufficient resources. It requires a structure where senior leaders can quickly make decisions regarding conflicts in areas such as contention across projects for key resources, development or testing environments, training rooms, and such.

Effectively managing the portfolio provides the needed information on the workload and projects to see the impact adding a change initiative will have.

Reflection Questions:

1. Does the organization have a clear understanding of what constitutes projects and programs?
2. Is there an effective portfolio management practice in place?
3. Are the project workloads aligned with the available resources and budget?
4. Is there governance in place to ensure alignment of work efforts across the organization?

CHAPTER 11

PROGRAM ORGANIZATION STRUCTURE

One of the most common mistakes I see when structuring a program is what appears to be a confusion between *functional* and *project* roles. Clarity and understanding which structure to use when and where is key to success.

While functional roles tend to lend themselves to matrix management, they aren't particularly effective for managing a large program, in my experience. For a program, which is a collection of related projects, having one overall program manager with project managers reporting into the program manager in a hierarchical structure works well.

I like to use a library analogy for staffing programs, where the people in the organization and books are analogous.

You go to your library and check out a book containing the information you desire for a specific amount of time. No one from the library comes to your house during that time asking to borrow the book for someone else—the book is dedicated to you for the specific time, sometimes with an option to renew.

YOU CONTROL THE BOOK

When staffing a program, the resources assigned from functional departments should be the people who have the requisite knowledge (remember, availability is not a skill!) and who can be assigned for the duration of time their expertise is needed, fully dedicated to the position without interruption. (We will talk more about backfilling resources under the staffing section.) This resource has been provided to the program manager who will work on the program, when the program or project manager provides the day-to-day direction.

The team members need to fully understand direction is given by the executive sponsor and program leadership—not by his or her functional manager.

It's not uncommon for a person assigned to a project to go to their functional manager if there is an issue or concern. This escalation is usually not helpful and creates unnecessary churn as now the functional manager who isn't working on the project decides to go to an executive who then goes to the program manager only to find that the issue is already being addressed. How efficient was that?

HAVE A PLAN... AND FOLLOW IT

The hierarchical program structure provides several benefits for effective execution. First, there are clearly defined reporting lines, from individual contributors to team leads to project managers to the program manager to the executive sponsor. This structure enables a clear escalation path when project issues arise. It supports clearly defined team roles to ensure work isn't missed or duplicated. Decision-making is more efficient since the buck stops with the program manager and executive sponsor.

For this or any program structure to work, the executive team must have confidence in the program manager and supporting leadership roles. Executives are usually impatient and want tasks to be done yesterday. As with a pregnancy, there is a gestation period for getting work done. A farmer doesn't wait until summer to plant crops and then wonder why there's no fall harvest. While gestation times in nature are known, we don't have the luxury of knowing how long gestation periods of the ideas and transformations will be.

HAVE TRUST IN YOUR PROCESS

However, there is a sequence of best practices to follow, allowing the team members to do their work. This is where the trust comes in. The program should be staffed with leaders who are proficient in their roles and trusted to develop the right approaches to take, staffing plans, schedules, and such. More on this in the scheduling section.

You may be wondering about the much-touted agile approach for delivery and how it fits into this picture. The program structure described above doesn't preclude the use of agile. For example, if a development manager wants developers to use agile and another one wants to use waterfall, that may be fine. If the team can set schedules and document requirements in a useful way to support program goals, and report progress in a consistent manner, it's usually acceptable for them to work however they want. The delivery approach may be set by the PMO or program manager, depending on a need for consistency or flexibility.

CAUTION

A word of caution—many software development teams use agile to cut corners, prototyping their way through. This is not how agile is intended to be used.

Here's an analogy of how agile is often implemented: Get in your car and start driving north on the nearest freeway. An hour later, you receive a call telling you to stop driving north and head east. After another few hours, another call comes in stating you should try heading south for a while.

The way agile is intended to be implemented should be more like this: We know we need to drive from Austin, TX to Albany, NY in the winter. A northeast direction is a given. We may need to course correct along the way due to construction, traffic, or weather, which may require significant deviations from a northeasterly direction, but we know the target we are supposed to hit. We may not know the exact address we need to go to early on, but it becomes clearer as we progress on our journey. See the difference?

Reflection Questions:

1. Has the initiative's organization structure been developed with clearly defined projects and support areas?
2. Are the roles and responsibilities clearly defined and communicated?
3. Do project team members understand the reporting structure?

CHAPTER 12

GO SLOW TO GO FAST

Many of us have seen the Dilbert cartoon that says, *"You start coding while I run upstairs and gather requirements,"* or a similar one. There is a tendency to have people start working because we know some of the steps will need to be taken.

Consider the similarities to building a house. Would you start to install appliances before the house has walls and floors? Before the interior reaches a certain point of completion? Starting to work before the vision is established and shared is like installing the dishwasher before the plumbing and electricity are in place.

There is a misperception that some work is better than no work and if teams are working, progress is being made. While taking time to establish and communicate the vision and the why may seem like it will slow down the momentum and process, it will pay off when everyone is aligned and moving in the same direction.

The same can be said for team-building activities. This helps with employee buy-in and reduces the resistance associated with change and uncertainty.

One of the least known areas is how much parallelism is possible in knowledge work. Because we are ambitious, we want to drive concurrent work. But there is a sequential nature to much of our work. The challenge is to find work that can be performed in parallel and then to be appropriately patient incorporating the sequential tasks.

Don't rush putting vendor contracts in place without proper scope and terms and conditions. Use attorneys who have the expertise to write good contracts. One of my clients, a large non-profit, used a pro bono attorney to develop a contract for a software solution to handle nationwide transactions.

A review of the contract, showed it heavily favored the vendor. It turned out the pro bono attorney's expertise was in harassment cases—not outsourcing software vendors. Clearly, putting in the necessary time to write good contracts using attorneys who have the right experience would have paid off for my client and will for you as well.

Hire the right people, even though it can be time-consuming. Put the right people on the bus who have the right attitudes and expertise, and the work will go much faster with far less drag on the teams. Take the time needed for developing the job description, interviewing candidates, and selecting high performers.

Spend the appropriate time to document the desired future-state processes to gain a good understanding of how it will be different in the future. Depending on the environment, you may need to document the current-state processes to more easily identify changes.

At a minimum, know what is directionally correct on what is needed up front versus deciding to figure it out as you go along. Defining the future state processes provides a foundation for gathering requirements for solutions, identifying where change will have the greatest impact, risk areas, and training needs.

Remember: *Never time to do it right, but always time to do it over...and over...and over.*

Reflection Questions:

1. Are we taking the necessary time to ensure we are putting processes in place to position the change initiative to be successful?
2. Are we working on procedures for the sake of doing something instead of ensuring it's the right task?
3. Have projects had to be redone where the rework could've been prevented had proper time been taken?

CHAPTER 13

STAKEHOLDERS

First, let's define what a stakeholder is: a stakeholder is a person (or group of people) who has an interest in or concern about the initiative.

This includes employees, customers, investors, suppliers, vendors, and maybe the community. Understanding why a stakeholder is interested is important. Will they be supportive or try to sabotage the efforts? One large program in the utility industry had over 200 stakeholders, where some were going to benefit, and some were going to lose. Managing the stakeholder group required a team of people to continue moving the program forward for the greater good. Being able to drive consensus with this group was no small feat.

If you understand the stakeholder interests and concerns upfront, you can better manage stakeholders who may be naysayers wanting to derail the initiative and leverage those who are supportive.

Managing stakeholders can be a full-time job for one or more people for large initiatives. Identify the stakeholders (individuals, groups) as well as the level of power and influence they have on the program. Develop an approach for increasing support and decreasing negative impacts. Monitor this on a regular basis to minimize surprises.

In some cases, engaging stakeholders as part of the decision-making process is critical to ensuring success. They may disagree with a decision, but if they were part of the process, they understand how the decision was made and why.

Reflection Questions:

1. Do I know who the stakeholders are and their interests?
2. What plan is in place for managing stakeholder requests?
3. Am I using an effective medium for keeping stakeholders informed?

CHAPTER 14

FINANCIAL PLANNING AND BUDGETING

D eciding the approach upfront for managing the financials of a program will save a lot of time and rework down the road. Determine what will be included in the program's budget and how the information will be collected. When capturing labor costs, do you need to include overhead and General and Administrative (G&A) costs as well?

Decide what will be capitalized and expensed and communicate these guidelines to the program or project managers. Also, determine how these costs will be collected, tracked, and reported in the accounting system (e.g., time tracking system, allocations, average salary costs vs. actual).

This is important for knowing how much has been spent against the budget, and for knowing how much has been spent against the amount of work performed.

For example, if a two-week task is budgeted to cost $4,000 in labor, but at the end of the first week, only 25 percent of the work has been completed, the task is going to cost more.

A good PMO leader will know how to use techniques such as Earned Value to track the amount of work performed against the budget to predict budget and schedule overruns (or underruns) early in the project life cycle. Government contracts require the use of Earned Value reporting on larger contracts, requiring integrated time-tracking systems and project schedules, which can be cumbersome in the commercial world.

There are lite approaches for using Earned Value that will provide directional correctness and early warning signals. A good master scheduler will implement an appropriate lite version to measure the work performed against work planned. It's important for program and project managers to work closely with the financial team to track work completed against the budget.

LARGE PROGRAMS

For large programs, consider setting up a financial management office (FMO) to oversee the program's financial systems, data collection, and reporting. At a minimum, the finance people should be working closely with the PMO to tie the work performed or planned, schedule, and budget into a cohesive reporting unit. Integrate the financial information into the overall program dashboard developed by the PMO.

When planning the budget, consider a contingency fund with governance structure for allocating funds to account for a change in scope, unknown issues, or valid reasons where additional funding is justified. By putting controls in place for allocating contingency funds, there is visibility into how quickly this money is being used and for what. This helps the program or project managers do a better job defining the budget and managing it as well as managing scope.

Reflection Questions:

1. Is there a defined approach for how to manage the financials of the change initiative?
2. Are the right controls and reporting in place for tracking the financials?
3. Is there a way to determine if the costs incurred are appropriate for work performed?

CHAPTER 15

SUPPORT ORGANIZATIONS

S ervices provided by support organizations are just as important for change initiatives as for the company overall, yet are often overlooked when planning the projects.

Engaging support functions, such as legal and compliance, finance, accounting, human resources, training, and development, early in the initiative saves a lot of time and headaches later.

COMPLIANCE

For those of us who are in highly regulated industries (and who isn't these days?), ensure representation from the compliance team from the start.

One client spent over $10M for a custom software solution only to find there was no record of who had entered or made changes to financial transactions – a requirement for auditing purposes. There were no archival requirements for storing transactions or audits. These oversights, along with other requirements missed, led to a messy years-long legal battle, where the only winners were the attorneys.

On another large program, the future-state processes had over 300 manual and exception processes. This would never have met compliance requirements, and luckily, the compliance department provided guidance on how to automate more of the processes and minimize exceptions to an acceptable level.

Special attention must be given to those change initiatives with technology components in addition to industry-specific rules and regulations.

For example, does your organization store customer data in the cloud? If so, your organization must meet System and Organization Control (SOC) compliance requirements. All public companies must comply with the Sarbanes-Oxley (SOX) Act for both the financial and IT side. Every industry seems to have its own seemingly endless list of regulatory requirements to meet.

Most organizations in regulated industries have compliance departments with qualified people to ensure that compliance requirements are met. The problem is the compliance folks are brought into the change initiative too late, resulting in rework.

Compliance requirements and processes are as important as the other requirements to be met. Include the compliance team in the stakeholder list upfront and enlist their help when developing business processes and requirements. It will save you a lot of time down the road.

HUMAN RESOURCES

Human Resources (HR) is another key department when it comes to change initiatives. This team must be a closely aligned and competent partner in the change initiative to help drive the desired results. Examples of HR contributions include the following:

Communications and Facilitation. With a clear understanding of the vision and direction, HR develops a communication plan and plays an instrumental role in cascading it from top to bottom throughout the organization. This team may facilitate critical meetings, such as town halls or other meetings where many people hear the message. Ensuring consistent messaging in well-run meetings goes a long way to minimize rumors and instill confidence in the leadership team.

Change Agent. The HR team needs to be a change agent for the initiative, constantly supporting and communicating the change and anticipating impacts and timing of the change. There should be a process for soliciting, evaluating, and integrating employee feedback.

Impact on Employees. There are impacts to the workforce with any change initiative, with some impacts being quite significant. HR determines how and to what extent each affected employee will be impacted and determines a course of action for each employee. The course of action may be to provide the employee with training to prepare them for a new role, or find another home for the employee within the organization, or work with them to find a new job outside the company if their skills are no longer required.

Staffing Plan. HR works with the leadership team to understand the staffing needs to support the change initiative during its implementation, and after, to develop a staffing plan. This includes:

- Inventory of current staffing and competencies
- Current and future-state staffing needs (gap analysis)

- Factors to influence staffing, such as low unemployment, difficulty finding people with unique skills, external workforce availability, trends and regulations
- Key employees who could be flight risks
- Headcount staffing
- Staffing composition (skills, contractors, employees)
- Sources for recruiting needed talent
- Need for backfilling key team members to enable their participation in and contribution to the change initiative.

Employee Retention. With change comes uncertainty, fear, and anxiety. Employees may start to look for opportunities with other companies, especially if they are concerned about their role once the changes have been implemented. When one person leaves, this causes others to consider looking around, especially if the person(s) who left is someone who was held in high regard in the company. HR must closely monitor this risk and be prepared to mitigate the situation with retention incentives. This could be in the form of retention bonuses paid out only if the employee stays during the needed time and performs at an appropriate level.

Talent Acquisition. HR is responsible for working with the leadership team to develop job descriptions for new or changed roles, identifying candidates to interview, putting together appropriate interview teams, and equipping the interview teams with appropriate interview questions.

Many companies have an ad hoc way of interviewing. The interview teams are based on who is available, and an interviewer is handed a resume. This results in different people asking the candidate the same questions (so, why are you interested in working here?). A good recruiter provides probing questions to each interviewer to gain more depth and breadth of the candidate's experience.

For example, what questions should someone be asking to determine if the candidate will be a cultural fit and who is responsible for asking these questions? What questions should be asked for situational and behavioral interviewing, and who is asking which questions?

Too often, hiring decisions are made on emotion and how well someone was liked instead of their skills. If your HR department isn't providing this level of recruiting professionalism, this would be a good time to upgrade your HR leader. Otherwise, it will be difficult to know if you're putting the right people on the bus.

One client, a large financial services company, had a highly effective HR department. They were committed to implementing a change initiative for over 4,000 people in the company. This initiative had a dedicated team of people who were highly experienced in organizational change management, whose role was to always be out in front of the change. This team was called the Change Awareness Team and was integral to the success of the initiative.

They were responsible for all the communications and keeping the initiative aligned from top to bottom. Team members were always a month or more ahead of the project teams, constantly letting employees know what was coming, why it was important, what training would be provided, and anticipating questions and providing answers in advance. This team provided all the functions described above and made the changes much easier to implement.

This is not to say all went smoothly and there was no resistance. However, the work done by this team made the job much easier. The change initiative was completed on schedule with the realized business value. I highly recommend having an experienced team like this lead organizational change aspects.

TRAINING AND MENTORING

The training team plays an essential role in change initiatives providing training for key roles across the company. Leadership training early in the initiative reminds leaders and managers of how they should lead their teams through this period of change and uncertainty. This is an optimal time to set expectations for leadership team behaviors and engagement.

Statistics show a third of management behavior does not support change, even when they understand the why. Having the leadership team and management on the same page regarding the change management process (not just the changes to be made but the process to follow to implement the changes) helps make them aware of behavior expectations. These are the people who need to set the examples for their teams. A leader's interaction with an employee who is confused about the transformation, doesn't support it, or questions it, becomes a moment of truth for the employee and the leader. These interactions either create momentum or drain it.

Setting the leadership expectations upfront helps provide the structure for holding teams accountable to their roles in the change initiative and process.

The training team partners with the change management team to develop a clear understanding of the change initiative.

They explain the why, the change management process, the stakeholders, who will be impacted by the changes, how the changes will affect employees and staff (internal and external), the expected (and unexpected) resistance areas, the early adopters, and subject matter experts who can help develop or deliver the training.

Armed with this information, the training team can determine the number of people who need to receive training, the breadth and depth of training, when to schedule the training, the best way to roll out the training, and how to measure its effectiveness.

Training needs may not be limited to internal staff. Be sure to include external stakeholders in the training needs assessment. Perhaps clients or vendors will need to work differently with your company. Points of contact may change, lines of communications may change, escalations may be different, and there may be new interfaces into portals.

MENTORING AMIDST CHANGE

Mentoring is equally as important as training when developing new capabilities across the organization.

Having someone who can answer questions and provide guidance to the teams once training has been completed reduces frustration and resistance and trying to circumvent the system. Training, paired with mentoring, provides the confidence needed when employees and other team members may have anxiety and fear about their ability to perform well in their new role.

The Change Awareness Team mentioned in the earlier example did a great job of identifying people who could serve as mentors and assigned them to staff members who had completed various training modules. They monitored each person's ability to perform the new job function(s) and worked to ensure each person was successful in his or her position.

FINANCE

Not involving finance early in the process can wreak havoc later. Business is all about the numbers. Having your finance partner engaged is paramount. The finance team is responsible for clearly defining tasks and processes like:

- Needed financial controls and security
- Separation of duties
- When to use charge codes and description
- How to track and record time
- What is included as costs or expenses to the change initiative versus normal operating costs
- How to take revenue (if applicable, to your change initiative)
- Financial reporting and key performance indicators
- How to measure the Return on Investment (ROI) of the change initiative.

More than one client decided the accounting codes in use for large programs were no longer sufficient and had to be redone. What a distraction and waste of time it is to ask employees to go back several months and change their time to different codes or to split it out differently.

As mentioned earlier, the finance department and PMO work closely together to determine if costs expended are in line with the amount of work getting done. Developing this level of information sharing allows the two groups to determine early in the initiative's life cycle if there are schedule or budget overruns.

LEGAL

An earlier chapter describes the need for having the right legal staff review and negotiate contracts.

Complex agreements should be developed using attorneys who specialize in the type of agreement needed. Far too many contracts are developed and signed by in-house attorneys or people in leadership roles resulting in vague or hard-to-enforce agreements. Terms and conditions were poorly written and Statements of Work (SOWs) were unclear in terms of the work required, schedules, deliverables, accountability, and similar important detail. Much gnashing of teeth can be avoided by spending the time upfront to get the right contracts in place. It makes it much easier, especially if it becomes necessary to litigate for non-performance.

Earlier I provided an example of a nonprofit organization using a pro bono attorney whose background was in employee harassment instead of outsourcing. As expected, the contract was terminated after the vendor had not met its obligations and it turned into a legal project.

A different law firm with experienced outsourcing attorneys was hired to represent the nonprofit. Ultimately, much of the money was paid back from the consulting firm who had been awarded the contract, but not before high costs had been incurred by the nonprofit's staff who had worked on the system and the legal fees. All of this could have been avoided had the nonprofit used counsel with outsourcing experience and hired a program manager to manage the program on their side.

Now that you have hired the right attorneys to develop the appropriate contracts, share these documents with the leadership team. Program and project managers, in particular, need to understand what the expectations are for all parties, including the client. Once contracts have been executed, the terms or conditions and statements of work should be reviewed by the leadership team.

The legal team explains roles and responsibilities of the vendor and client, deliverables, invoicing, and such. Leaders should have a solid understanding of this information to hold all parties accountable.

The legal department usually has responsibility for monitoring contracts, expiration dates, expenditures against the contract, and determining when or if contract extensions or modifications are required. If your change initiative requires several vendors, having a vendor manager may be a useful role. This person works closely with the PMO to understand vendor progress, relays contract terms to the project managers, and ensures the vendors are providing the contracted services.

I've worked on both the side of the client and the side of the vendor when there were contract disputes—it's not fun any way you look at it. Lots of time and money are expended in building legal cases against the other side, time that could've been spent doing more productive work had the contracts been written better from the beginning and clear expectations set.

Reflection Questions

1. Do I have representatives from compliance on the teams to provide requirements?

2. Is my HR leader engaged and capable of providing the staffing needs, support for change management, and needed communications?

3. Have my contracts been thoughtfully developed and executed by those who have the requisite skills?

4. Is my training leader engaged and capable of providing the training needed?

5. Are my finance and project teams working closely together to provide insights on budget and schedule performance?

IMPLEMENTATION: READY—AIM—FIRE

"Planning without action is futile;
action without planning is fatal."
~ Cornelius Fichtner

CHAPTER 16

PROGRAM KICK-OFF MEETING

We've spent time putting everything in place to improve the chances the change initiative will be successful; now we're ready to start implementing the work. If you are thinking, *"That WAS a lot of work to get here!"*, you are absolutely correct. It's the effort applied to this point that should give you confidence in a successful outcome.

Abraham Lincoln said, *"Give me six hours to chop a tree and I will spend the first four sharpening the axe."*

One of my colleagues runs marathons, and he will tell you the training is always more difficult than the race. You put in a lot of miles to do well on race day.

This isn't to imply everything must be in place for the entire change initiative—that would be a bit overwhelming. But we should have a pretty good game plan in place by now and be ready to start executing on the plan.

The purpose of the program kickoff meeting is to set the foundation to position the program to be successful by setting clear expectations. It provides an opportunity for everyone to be on the same page. The amount of time required for this varies based on the number of people who need to be informed, the complexity of the initiative, the amount of information for dissemination, and such.

Kickoff meetings may last for a few hours to several days. They may be spread over several times, depending on how the initiative is structured.

The program kick-off meeting is not the type of meeting where an email is recommended to communicate the approach. Take the time needed to organize and plan the meeting. Today, the various methods of communication make this much easier with video conferencing and recordings. Allow time for questions, possibly collecting them in advance.

Suggested topics to include as part of the kick-off meeting include:

- Introductions
- Purpose of the initiative
- Why the initiative is important to the company
- Desired outcomes of the initiative
- How success will be measured
- Scope (what's in scope as well as what's out of scope)
- Key deliverables
- Risks
- How the program will be planned and managed
- Expectations for engagement (e.g., if a key resource is assigned full time to the program, the manager can't keep pulling him or her back)
- Roles and responsibilities
- Staffing—backfill resources, consulting partners and their roles
- Program organization structure and reporting chain
- Vendors and their roles

- A program roadmap with key milestones and target completion dates
- Deliverables and the approval process
- Collaboration (what tools will be used)
- Escalation when there are issues.

Be sure to assign someone to take notes during the meeting, capturing key points and action items for follow-up. If you don't write it down, it never happened. Everyone should leave the meeting with a good understanding of what comes next and his or her role.

Reflection Questions

1. Have I prepared well for the kickoff meeting(s) required to get the teams aligned with the work to be performed?
2. Does everyone understand their individual and team roles?
3. Were clear and realistic expectations set during the kickoff meeting?

CHAPTER 17

OUTSOURCING OR CONTRACTING

I t's not uncommon to contract for outside services to perform portions of the work associated with the transformation. This may include hiring consulting firms to lead the effort, or outsourcing firms for software development and testing, or resources to backfill roles.

Consultants and outsourcing services provide guidance on organizational change management, develop business processes, and provide specialized knowledge not held within the company.

In any of these cases, the legal staff drafting the contracts should have expertise in outsourcing and consulting agreements. Where possible, contracts should have incentives and penalties based on vendor performance. Take the time needed to ensure clearly written statements of work to provide as much clarity as possible. If internal legal counsel doesn't have the requisite skills for outsourcing agreements, hire a firm that does. It will save a lot of headaches and money later.

SELECTING THE RIGHT VENDOR

If there are multiple vendors that can provide the services or solutions requested, sending Requests for Proposals (RFPs) to vendors to elicit proposal responses is prudent for receiving the best pricing for the level of service or solution proposed. New ideas are often presented that may not have been considered before.

Negotiations with multiple vendors upfront are usually more effective than negotiating with a single vendor.

Insights into the capabilities of vendors not selected provide a fallback position in the event the vendor chosen fails to perform.

The legal staff provides guidance on the best type(s) of contract to use along with incentives and penalties for performance. There are numerous contract types to choose from, and it's important to select the right one for the type of work to be performed.

For example, working under a fixed-price statement of work requires both parties to complete deliverables by a specified time. If the client doesn't provide the services or needed information in a timely manner, the vendor will likely submit a change order asking for schedule relief and more money.

This brings up another point on picking the right kind of agreement: fixed price, not-to-exceed, or time and materials.

Fixed-priced agreements may be used when the work is well understood and has been done before. Vendors tend to push back on these, and oftentimes will inflate estimates to absorb overruns since all risk is on the vendor.

Not-to-exceed agreements are used to control costs where a vendor bills for services rendered up to the not-to-exceed amount. After that, the vendor is obligated to finish the work without additional pay. This isn't a common arrangement since the vendor has no upside if the work is completed early.

Time-and-material agreements allow the vendor to charge hourly rates that are negotiated upfront and bill on a regular basis for time worked and any expenses incurred, such as travel. These agreements need to be managed carefully to ensure accountability.

Part of the PMO's role may include vendor management by providing vendor oversight and assisting project managers to ensure deliverables are submitted in a timely manner and of sufficient quality.

Reflection Questions:

1. Do I have a clear understanding of why a vendor is needed and the services they will provide?
2. How will I manage vendor performance?
3. What happens if a vendor fails to perform in accordance with their contract?
4. Was the vendor contract structured with the proper legal support?

CHAPTER 18

PROGRAM MANAGEMENT OFFICE (PMO)

For those of you who are Darren Hardy (author of *The Compound Effect*) fans, you know one of his principles is to *"Do now, so you never have to do again."* This means you set up the project correctly the first time. A carpenter who needs to cut a lot of boards the same length doesn't measure every board and then cut each individually. Instead, a jig is built ensuring every board is cut easily and precisely in bulk without much thought needed.

Think of the PMO as the entity responsible for determining the jigs needed and then building them for ease of use and standardization. Professionals who have the requisite experience to understand the cross-functional and delivery complexities inherent in large programs should be assigned or hired to build them.

If there is an existing PMO in the organization, confirm it is staffed with people who have the requisite skills to manage a large, complex initiative. Many organizations have PMOs in place to manage traditional projects. These may be ill-equipped to manage large, complex change initiatives. It is not uncommon to stand up a PMO specifically to provide the overall management and oversight of a large initiative and then dissolve it after completion.

Large initiatives are like transformation puzzles. Understanding how the pieces of the puzzle fit together will optimize the delivery of the desired transformation. The PMO defines all the projects and workstreams for a large program and determines what dependencies they have on each other.

One common mistake is to start as many projects upfront as possible. On one failing program every project had been started (all 17 of them), including an enterprise data warehouse project where several million dollars had been spent without even knowing what the data sources were, what data was needed, and what data would be captured. This resulted in significant rework once the other projects containing the data sources caught up.

Just because a project *can* be started doesn't mean it *should* be. Eli Goldratt's book, ***The Goal***, is a great read for understanding the theory of constraints, bottlenecks, and how to optimally sequence work.

PMO STRUCTURE

PMO structures can take several shapes.

I like to have the PMO reporting into the overall program executive with the project managers reporting to the PMO. This ensures consistency in how work is accomplished and provides a single point of accountability with the PMO leader. Other roles in the PMO include master scheduling, risk and issue management, process standardization, systems or tools, program controls, financial reporting, and vendor management. Depending on the size of the initiative, each of these roles could be one person or multiple people.

ROLES IN THE PMO

The PMO has a lot of work streams or projects to coordinate and manage for change initiatives. This section describes key roles commonly housed in a PMO tasked with managing a large, complex program accompanying change initiatives.

PMO Leader. This individual must have expertise in building and managing PMOs that have been successful in other programs of a similar size and complexity to your change initiative. Building a PMO and managing a PMO are two different functions—sort of like the difference between the architect designing your house and someone living in it. This person should understand how the puzzle pieces fit together and know how to build the supporting project delivery infrastructure. The PMO leader may be the difference between success or failure of the change initiative.

Project Managers. The project managers lead each project of the change initiative. They should have experience managing projects that are cross-functional in nature. As mentioned earlier, the complexity of managing cross-functional projects is much higher than managing a self-contained project within a department. (Remember complexity vs. complicated?)

Master Scheduler. Hiring one or more master schedulers is a common practice for large government programs but not so much for commercial programs. I find having a master scheduler(s) is a necessity for integrating project schedules for cross-functional dependencies, maintaining the proper level of detail, identifying the critical path or near-critical paths through the initiative, and identifying changes when there are slips in the various schedules.

Don't confuse a project manager with a master scheduler. Just because someone says they have used MS Project or Smartsheets doesn't mean they are a master scheduler. Ask them to provide sample of baselined integrated program schedules and the types of analysis they run against them during the interview.

On one large initiative, I asked the previous program manager for the project schedules. He said the program was too large and complex to use a project management tool—the only way to manage it was using slide decks and spreadsheets. For a moment, I thought, *He's trying to be funny, but I don't get the joke.*

He was liberatead back to the job market and two master schedulers brought onto the program worked with the PMs to develop an integrated program schedule, complete with cross-project dependencies, critical or near-critical paths, and reporting based on real data which was used until the program was successfully completed.

The schedule had well over 10,000 tasks, and everyone had visibility into the deliverables on the critical path. Each team on the critical path knew the focus was on them, and extra attention and resources were provided to keep the work on schedule.

Today, I wouldn't even consider leading a large, complex program without a master scheduler. Once you've worked with a good one, this will be one of the first roles you fill. It's like a smart phone—after you've had one, you keep it nearby!

Risk and Issue Manager. Having one person responsible for working with project managers on risks and issues is immensely helpful. Too often, risk and issue management becomes a check box exercise where the risks and issues are documented but that's about it.

Important high-risk areas and mitigation plans are reported on in a consistent manner. This person is responsible for ensuring mitigation tasks are incorporated into the appropriate project schedules. I worked on one global program where the mitigation plan for the adoption of a software solution for a large client in Europe had as many tasks as the implementation component of the program in the US. Don't underestimate the time it takes for mitigation activities and incorporate these activities into the overall schedule.

PMO Process Expert. The person in this role ensures processes are developed and followed consistently. For example, this person is responsible for developing processes such as the requirements management process, scope change management process, estimation process, risk and issue process, escalation process, and such. Ensuring each process is being consistently followed is equally important. Sometimes a Quality Assurance person may have responsibility for ensuring PMO process compliance.

PMO Trainer. A designated trainer is invaluable as new people and projects come onboard. This role ensures new team members are ramped up quickly and productive on all the relevant processes, procedures, and tools that are being used. PMO-related questions are frequently directed to the PMO Trainer. This role provides guidance on how to use the project management software, how requirements are gathered and traced, the templates to use for documenting business processes, how estimation is done, what is required for status reporting, where documentation is stored, and other project management functions.

Administrative Support. There is a lot of information to be collected and managed as well as meetings to be scheduled for the projects associated with a change initiative. This may be one or more people, depending on what help is required by the other PMO staff members.

Standard Process, Guidelines, Deliverables

A key function of the PMO is standardizing processes, guidelines, tools, and deliverables across the initiative (building jigs). This ensures:

- Business process work and requirements are developed in a consistent manner.
- Templates are consistent across the look and feel of deliverables and tasks like how-to version documents guarantee everyone knows which documents are the final ones, which are works in progress, and which should be archived.
- Standard processes are in place to provide consistency and avoid overlap or missing tasks for up or downstream work. Process such as requirements gathering, managing estimation reporting, risk and issue management, testing, and escalation are examples in need of standardization. Team members should simply complete forms instead of developing their own documentation which could interfere with putting the puzzle together efficiently.
- Status reporting is done uniformly across projects and rolled up into overall program dashboards, and includes the status of items like work performed, financial

information, and resource management. Developing status report templates to meet the reporting needs of the program manager, executives, and board members takes a lot of effort. Making sure this is correct upfront saves a lot of time reworking it later.

- Risk and issue gathering and management are done and reported on consistently. Establishing definitions of high, medium, and low risk or issue definitions upfront, with examples, will make it easier for project managers and team members to accurately document and mitigate risks and issues.

- Documentation is stored in the right repositories with proper file naming conventions and versioning.

MEETING EFFICIENCY

Meetings scheduled and managed by the PMO should be run efficiently and effectively as these meetings usually have attendees from multiple functional areas and require cross-functional information dissemination and decision-making.

Some meetings will require a meeting cadence, such as bi-weekly status meetings. These recurring meetings are determined by the PMO as to what meetings are needed, the purpose of the meeting, who should attend, how often these meetings should occur, and the best medium for holding the meeting (e.g., in-person, web meetings, conference calls). These recurring meetings are scheduled in advance to ensure the time is blocked on the meeting participants' calendars.

PMO meetings may benefit by using a skilled facilitator to work with the appropriate people to develop meeting agendas, distribute relevant meeting information to participants, set meeting expectations, and facilitate the meeting to keep it focused and on track. A person should be assigned for documenting the meeting minutes, any decisions reached, and action items to follow up on prior to the next meeting.

CENTRALIZED DOCUMENTATION REPOSITORY

Another key function of the PMO is establishing a centralized repository for collecting, maintaining, and archiving program documentation.

I've been in companies where they proudly proclaim they use data repositories, like SharePoint, Jira, Google, or OneDrive, to store documentation. When you dig into the details, there could be hundreds of unorganized, duplicate folders. It is difficult to know what is current, still used, or should be archived. There are multiple document graveyards existing because someone said, "Let's throw this in folders."

One client had accumulated over 1,000 SharePoint directories with no documentation as to what was current and what wasn't. The team had to add a workstream to go through the files to determine which ones were still relevant and move the remaining files into an archive.

Whether you're starting an initiative from the beginning or recovering an existing one, make sure you include the work necessary to setup a well-organized repository with the proper security controls, file-naming conventions, and version control and team members understand how to use it.

COLLABORATION TOOLS

Collaboration tools are established for use across teams, ensuring reliable means for communicating consistently. These are even more critical as more and more work is done remotely.

A few examples of the areas for collaboration tools include:

- Project Management. Assign tasks to team members, report progress consistently against the tasks, and track risks, issues or notes associated with tasks or projects.

- Business Processes. Document business processes. Make them available for review and consumption of the appropriate team members.

- Requirements Gathering or Management. Select a requirements tool that supports feedback, questions, and responses, baselining the requirements and managing changes to scope. It is helpful to select a requirements management tool that integrates with an automated testing tool. This makes it much easier to understand which test cases apply to specific requirements and if the test cases pass or fail.

- Team Communications. Choose a chat or instant messaging tool to enable team members easy access to each other to quickly ask questions or relay information.

- Web Meetings. The number of people who work remotely continues to increase, especially in today's world. It is a necessity to have a reliable solution for hosting meetings virtually, video conferencing, and screen sharing.

- Knowledge Base. The rate at which information is generated grows exponentially. A searchable knowledge base to house the information where people can easily access it is invaluable for having one source of record accessible by all.

Training on the Jigs

In addition to collaboration tools, project templates, and repositories, each organization has standards for office software products, expense reporting systems, accounting systems, time-tracking systems, and other specialized software products.

Learning how to use all this software (which, by the way, is supposed to save us time) can be daunting. Most everyone will need training on how to use one or more of these tools. Take the time upfront to provide the jig training—doing this will save a lot of time downstream.

Have you been in a situation where you or others on your team have moved from an MS Office environment to GSuite? Go through the training— it will save a lot of frustration and swearing.

Reflection Questions:

1. Is a PMO set up to effectively manage and report on the change initiative?
2. Does the PMO provide reporting showing the information needed for decision-making?
3. What are the PMO tracking, reporting, and mitigating risks and issues?
4. Is the PMO proactive in escalating issues needing executive attention?

CHAPTER 19

PLANNING

If you've read this far (thank you!), you are aware planning is needed in a multitude of areas before the kickoff meeting.

This section focuses on the planning aspects of the overall initiative. The planning phase is where much of the heavy lifting occurs—this is where you build the foundation to support delivery. There is a natural flow, if implemented correctly, which allows the work to build on itself.

REQUIREMENTS GATHERING

Requirements gathering is a logical first place to start. There are several items to consider when selecting the approach for this.

For example, if part of the initiative is to implement a commercial software platform, it may make more sense to change the organization's business processes to conform to what is supported by the software, rather than to require extensive customization of the software that will be time-consuming and costly.

Configuring the software with minimal customizations to meet your business needs is usually the best approach.

Where It All Begins

The foundation to understanding requirements is to document current-state business processes, capturing manual as well as automated workflow. Processes are commonly documented using swim lanes with associated roles.

Be sure people assigned to document business processes are experts who understand how to do this work. It's not uncommon to see detailed flowcharts with systems embedded when it should be represented as processes from the business perspective, system agnostic.

Develop the future state business processes that document the to-be workflows and associated roles. The future state processes may be dictated somewhat by the vendor solution being implemented. The vendor should be able to provide this information or, at a minimum, a good starting point.

The current state and future state processes provide the foundation. If there are significant differences in skills required for the future state, this is a good time to include the HR team to determine the best way to upskill the existing workforce or plan for hiring the talent. It's the foundation for gathering more detailed requirements, which in turn serves as the foundation for developing test cases and user training. Don't confuse using an agile approach for implementation as a substitute for requirements gathering.

Assigning professional Business Analysts (BA) to do the requirements gathering will make life easier down the road.

BSs are worth every penny because they take a systematic approach to gathering business and user requirements and decompose these into more functional (how the user wants the system to work) and non-functional requirements (system performance, capacity, compliance). If possible, choose a requirements management tool with an integrated testing tool. This allows traceability from requirements to test cases and scenarios, accelerating the ability to complete testing more quickly with more coverage. The investment and training upfront will save a lot of time downstream.

CHANGE WITHIN COMPLEX SYSTEMS

Let me give you an example from a large program in the energy sector. The purpose of this initiative was to redesign how the electricity grid was planned, managed, and settled. Changes had to be compliant with hundreds of requirements set by regulatory entities.

We took the time upfront to develop a tracing strategy and to select a requirements management tool to support the compliance and requirements needs of the initiative. Each high-level requirement was linked (traced) to more detailed requirements, processes, procedures, and training, which in turn were all linked to test cases and test case scenarios. By having this tool, it was easy to determine the impact a scope change request might have.

For example, one change request had the potential to affect over 100 downstream requirements, over 10,000 test scenarios, and numerous training modules. A tool such as this allows the team to make informed decisions as to whether a change is really, really, really something that is needed.

In highly regulated areas, using a requirements management tool may prove compliance by linking regulatory requirements to system functionality, business processes, training, and operational procedures. Developing this trace strategy upfront will save a lot of time (and potential fines) later.

The agile practitioners sometimes argue that requirements gathering will be too time-consuming—they want to develop user stories and start coding. We find development groups think prototyping and user stories should be all that is needed. While this may work in some instances, this type of work still needs to be coordinated and managed across the initiative.

Risk and Issue Identification, Management

Throughout the lifecycle of the initiative, risks and issues should be identified, documented, assigned ownership, reported on, and mitigated.

The difference between a risk and an issue is the risk has a probability associated with it of less than 100 percent.

An issue is already identified as a concern with a 100 percent probability of happening. Robert Charette says, *"An issue is a risk whose time has come."*

There are many categories of risks. Here are a few:
- Adoption of the changes
- Information technology
- Information management
- Resource management
- Financial management
- Regulatory
- Compliance
- Legal
- Conflicts of interest
- Training
- Operational
- Knowledge management

- Political
- Privacy or information stewardship.

As mentioned earlier, It's helpful to assign an experienced person from the PMO to work across the program to gather and manage risks and issues. This ensures consistency in writing the risks and issues, identification of the work associated with managing the risks and issues for inclusion in the proper project schedule, and then relentless follow up on the mitigation plans.

Structure of a Risk and Issue. A risk or issue statement has two parts: the condition (phrase or sentence briefly describing the situation causing concern) and the consequence (phrase or sentence describing the possible outcomes).

Additional information about the risk can be provided as needed to add context. Here are examples of risk statements with the condition and consequence:

- Slowness of adoption of the new processes and systems may cause erosion of the business value associated with the change initiative.
- Delays in contract negotiations may cause the schedule to slip, which will increase costs.
- New regulations may result in significant rework, increasing costs, and extending the schedule.

Issues are stated similarly to risks with the exception the statement reflects the probability of occurrence is 100 percent.

For example, if we look at the risks above, they would be rewritten as issues as follows:

- Slow adoption of new processes and systems is eroding the business value expected from the change initiative.

- Delays in contract negotiations have caused the schedule to slip, and additional costs are being incurred.
- The new regulations require significant rework, which is increasing costs and extending the schedule.

RISK AND ISSUE IDENTIFICATION

Identifying risks and issues can be approached in a few ways. One is to have the assigned risk or issue manager meet with each team and facilitate a meeting to identify the risks and issues associated with their project(s).

Another is to use a risk taxonomy listing the common categories of risks associated with the work to be performed as part of the change initiative. The risk or issue manager may start with the categories of risks (such as those listed above) to provide a mechanism for focusing the teams on specific types of risks and issues.

As risks and issues are identified, the risk or issue manager documents them in a risk or issue statement in a centralized log the team can access.

Gathering and documenting risks and issues is not a one-and-done activity. It is ongoing throughout the change initiative and should be kept current.

MITIGATING RISKS OR ISSUES

Once risks and issues have been identified and documented, each should have a mitigation strategy on how to avoid or minimize the impact. Note that work associated with the mitigation strategies can be significant and must be accounted for in the overall program or project schedule.

SCHEDULE DEVELOPMENT

For large, complex transformations, developing a detailed schedule from start to finish is nearly impossible. There will likely be many changes and course corrections along the way as more information becomes available.

However, this doesn't mean a high-level schedule can't be developed and managed-to. Keeping the end in mind, a roadmap for how to get there can be developed, and detailed schedules can be developed for the early phases or iterations.

This is called rolling wave planning, where details are added as more and more information is known.

When dealing with software development teams using an agile approach, a rule of thumb is the team has at least two to four well-defined sprints where the functionality to be delivered is well known and documented. Another two to three months of work should be planned at a high level.

Tasks for each project or workstream are usually facilitated by the project manager and team members. Task granularity should be at a level where one person or a small team of people has responsibility for completion. Work to be done in the future where requirements aren't well known yet may be a larger block of time.

Once the tasks are documented, they are linked together to form a network diagram, showing dependencies across all of them. Some tasks will have to finish before others can start.

For example, before end-to-end integration testing can be started, system integrations must be completed. Knowing what work can be done in parallel will help determine the schedule as well as staffing needs.

The network diagram will aid in developing the critical path through each project to determine the overall duration of the program. Anything slipped on the critical path will slip the end date.

Once the tasks are identified and linked, the resources and skills needed can be considered. The project manager, HR, and procurement may need to work together to hire employees, contractors, or outsource the requisite skills.

ESTIMATION

There are many ways to estimate the duration and effort for projects and tasks. Two common categories of estimation are: sizing estimates and detailed estimates.

- Sizing estimates are used early in the project's lifecycle when there isn't as much detail. We may know we are going to implement a large software system, and the vendor provides information that it takes an average of 12 months to document processes, gather requirements, install the software, migrate the data, test in parallel, and then cut over—with a few caveats and assumptions along the way. This would be an example of a sizing estimate where analogous information is being used.

- Detailed estimates occur when the work is broken down into specific tasks (user stories for agile development), and the estimates are more granular. Where possible, have the person who will be doing the work provide the estimates. This ensures he or she buys into the time and effort required and is willing to be held accountable.

SCHEDULE REFINEMENT

A realistic schedule provides insights into the velocity of work completion, how slippages are impacting other related work, and key milestones.

In many situations, this is where the executive team says the schedule is too long and dictates a new schedule date, with little regard for the hard work completed to develop the schedule.

A better approach is to understand how the schedule was developed, the basis for estimates, and determine what trade-offs can be made to shorten the schedule.

For example:

- Can added resources effectively shorten the schedule?
- Can additional work be outsourced?
- Should something be bought vs. built?
- Can the program be phased, or the scope reduced?
- What distractions can be removed?
- Should teams co-locate to improve communications?
- What talent can be added to reduce the learning curves?

Rather than imposing dates (most are never hit and only cause frustration and burnout), perhaps an approach offering stretch goals and team rewards for delivering early is a more effective solution.

Iterate with the teams until a schedule is agreed to by all parties.

In the long run, rewards will encourage employee engagement, teamwork, and focus.

Reflection Questions:

1. Have the current and future state business processes been mapped?
2. Have the proper resources gathered requirements in a way that is understandable by the appropriate teams?
3. Is the overall schedule based on the requirements?
4. Are the tasks documented and linked to provide a high-level schedule for the initiative?

CHAPTER 20

STAFFING

Would you ask someone to fly you and your family across the country in a jet when their only experience piloting is flying drones and playing Flight Simulator? It's the same for large, complex programs.

When staffing a large program, there are several decisions to make:

- Do the requisite skills currently exist in the organization? (Be honest!)
- If not, are these skills you want to build in the organization?
- Who should be on the leadership team and do they have the requisite skills?
- What actions need to be taken to free up the best people to work on the program?

Key roles need to be staffed with the best people in the organization; not only people who are available. There are too many pieces to put together to hope people figure it out, even if they've been successful on a smaller scale.

Let's start with the leadership team. We've already talked about executive sponsorship and leadership skills. The next layers down are equally important. The program and project managers (PMs) need to have experience managing complex projects. There is a project management inflection point where many PMs fail. A PM may have a great track record running standalone projects (complicated) but fail spectacularly when trying to manage cross-functional projects (complex).

When you have a critical program, this is not the time to let someone sink or swim, even if they volunteer because they see it as an opportunity for career growth.

One quite effective approach is two-in-the-box, where an expert (perhaps an outside consultant) is put into the role and paired up with an employee who has the potential to grow into the role. The expert mentors the employee through the learning curve, and over time the knowledge is transferred to the employee, who has a safety net when making decisions or questions arise. This approach is recommended for all key roles where skills need to be developed.

When using a consulting company to help with the work and training, include knowledge transfer tasks as a specific part of the contract with deliverables to ensure your team can sustain the work.

AVOIDING MISTAKES

A common staffing mistake is expecting someone to somehow fit this into their day job. If they could manufacture time, they wouldn't be working for you—they'd make their billons and retire.

Think about which roles need to be backfilled and start this process in the earliest stages of the program. Backfill positions to free up the high-performing team members. This is much more likely to result in buy-in from the teams and allow them to focus on high-value work for the changes. Backfilling will likely take time to find the right people and should be started well in advance of a critical workstream.

As my friend and colleague, Dr. Joyce Statz would say, *"Availability is not a skill!"*

The people being used in a backfill role must have the requisite skills and are not just those who can be available. If extensive training is required, there may be a need to bring people in to backfill roles early in the initiative's lifecycle. On one large program, more than 40 subject matter experts were backfilled by contractors. This created a training window to allow the team time to learn how new systems and processes would work. Once the program was complete, the contractors were released.

Work with HR to develop an overall staffing plan to ensure the right people are in place when needed and the right mix of employees, contractors, vendors, and consultants are used to minimize the need for layoffs after the work is completed.

Frequently, people are assigned to multiple projects or work streams. This may be unavoidable if only one person has the requisite skills and supports multiple areas (which is common with Subject Matter Experts). Studies show a knowledge work must work 60 hours per week if assigned to two projects to have 20 hours of productivity on each. The more a person can be dedicated to a project for longer periods of time, the better.

Question anyone who supports effective multitasking or who expects knowledge workers to switch back and forth multiple times a day.

There is no such thing as multitasking on multiple cognitive workstreams! We can do multiple tasks when only one is cognitive and others are learned behaviors. For example, we can talk (using our hands-free devices) and drive a car simultaneously because driving the car is something we can do on autopilot. When trying to do two (or more) cognitive tasks simultaneously, we are really task-switching, sometimes referred to as a weapon of mass distraction.

The task at hand, and the people you interact with, deserve your full attention. A 5-minute distraction takes 25 minutes to get back to the same level of cognitive concentration a person had before the distraction.To the extent possible, assign people full time to positions requiring full-time attention.

Reflection Questions:

1. Do I have the right people for the work they are assigned?
2. Has the workload of the key team members been adjusted to allow for the time needed to support this initiative?
3. Have I backfilled key positions where team members are required full time on the initiative?

SUSTAINABILITY—MANAGE, MEASURE, AND ADJUST

"If you cannot measure it, you cannot control it."
~ Lord Kelvin

CHAPTER 21

MONITORING

Monitoring a program is the process of tracking and reporting on the critical aspects such as schedule, budget, staffing, scope management, and risk and issue management.

This provides an accurate status at a given point in time and provides information for use in identifying trends. For example:

- Is the schedule continuing to slip, or have the corrective actions started to take effect?
- Are the scope change requests increasing or decreasing?
- Are the risks and issue mitigation strategies working?
- Do we have the right number of people with the requisite skills?
- Are delays on one project adversely impacting another?
- Is the work completed in line with what was budgeted?

Program dashboards are established by the PMO and updated on a regular basis. Even though we've already talked about the role and importance of a PMO, it warrants repeating here. Consistent reporting across the program is crucial for program dashboards to be reliable. The project managers all need to be consistent in these areas:

- Planning projects
- Building project schedules
- Reporting on risks and issues
- Running meetings
- Tracking action items
- Escalating issues
- Estimating work
- Managing scope
- Status reporting.

The program or project management system needs to be in place at the very beginning of the initiative. Spend the time upfront to do this correctly and instill the discipline, and it will save countless hours of frustration later.

Determine how often you will provide updates to the Executive Steering Committee and make the meetings mandatory. The cadence may range from weekly to monthly. Work with the PMO leader to establish a program or project dashboard providing the committee the information it needs to evaluate the progress of the initiative.

More often than not, large programs have significant schedule slippages and budget overruns. In fact, some reports show this happens to over 80 percent of large programs.

If you're managing to a schedule, one option is reducing scope by either eliminating it entirely or deferring it to a later time. When scope is eliminated, and costs increase, it's a good time to review the business case for the initiative again. Is it still providing the business value and the return on investment (ROI) justifying it in the first place?

MORE IS NOT BETTER

It's common to add more resources when the schedule starts slipping. In Fred Brooks' classic book, **The Mythical Man Month**, Brooks' Law states, *"Adding manpower to a late software project makes it later."*

Adding people takes time for interviewing candidates, onboarding and training them, and increases the number of lines of communication required. Perhaps the problem isn't the number of people assigned to a project but rather poorly gathered requirements, changes to requirements, inaccurate estimates, unrealistic deadlines, wrong skills on the project team, or pulling the people assigned to the project back to other projects.

Increasing the number of people to solve a schedule problem is seldom the answer and only exacerbates the situation. As course corrections are needed, take the time to understand the root cause and adjust accordingly.

Reflection Questions:

1. Do I have enough status information to determine how the change initiative work is progressing, where there are problem areas, and where executive attention is required?

2. Are there regularly scheduled meetings with the senior leadership team for reviews?

3. Are project audits or reviews scheduled to ensure the accuracy of the processes and information presented?

CHAPTER 22

SCOPE MANAGEMENT

A s mentioned earlier, defining the scope sets the boundaries of a program, including what is not in scope as well as what is.

The scope definition defines and describes all work necessary to produce the program goals, allowing the people responsible for achieving it to understand their role.

With that said, scope change is inevitable, especially in large programs where more and more details are revealed as work progresses. This needs to be carefully managed and controlled with the appropriate governance structure in place. It's easy to get caught up in the *nice to have* mindset, causing delays and modifications.

Managing scope is one of the more challenging aspects of a large transformation program. Early in my career, I worked on a program to build an accounting system to consolidate 14 accounting systems across multiple naval locations.

Over 30 people were assigned to the government oversight team, whose primary purpose was to manage the scope, handle scope change requests, review and either approve or reject them. The program was canceled after audits by the General Accounting Office (GAO) reported the total lifecycle costs originally estimated in the $90M range had grown to $800M in a five-year period. Even with a dedicated team focused on scope management, scope creep had run rampant—our taxpayer dollars at work.

One of the inherent problems with changes in scope is the teams responsible for doing the work must stop to do an impact and cost analysis, delaying the work being completed and the schedule. Where there are lots of stakeholders, this can become especially problematic. Establish a Change Control Board (CCB) upfront to minimize the amount of time spent analyzing scope changes.

On the program mentioned earlier for redesigning the electricity grid, a filter was added to the CCB to stop any change not directly impacting reliability of the grid. On this program, vendors started charging for change request analyses and schedule relief because of the amount of time they were spending to research and estimate the changes. Over $100M in change requests were deferred until after *go-live*. This governance oversight and holding firm to only those necessary changes made the difference between success and failure.

Members of the CCB are those who have the authority and leadership skills to make the right decisions. They ask the right questions and engage the appropriate level of subject matter experts to provide sufficient information for decision-making. Impacts on other projects and workstreams within the program need to be carefully vetted. Often a change or new functionality seems like a great idea for one project only to find out it breaks something else.

In an effectively run CCB, the squeaky wheel's requests are fairly evaluated for what is in the best interest of the program. Change requests have a big ripple effect if approved. The PMO should be aware of all approved changes and ensure schedules and cross-functional dependencies are taken into consideration, and that documentation related to business processes or procedures, requirements, and test cases can be reflected.

A word of caution when dealing with scope changes at the requirements level: if there are a lot of change requests coming, it could be because the scope definition was not clear and requirements were poorly developed.

This came up on a program where the program manager (the same one who said the program was too big and complex to manage with PM software) said there was no time for gathering requirements. Can you imagine telling a builder to go out to your property and start nailing boards together to build your dream house? If you see a lot of requirements churn, it's probably time for a reset to get everyone on the same page.

Reflection Questions

1. Are there baselined requirements changes can be submitted against?
2. Is an effective Change Control Board in place for managing change requests?
3. Are there defined criteria for deciding when a change is approved or rejected?

CHAPTER 23

COMMUNICATIONS

T he need for frequent communications has been discussed throughout this book—its importance cannot be emphasized enough. *Communicate. Communicate. Communicate.*

Assign a person (or team, depending on complexity) to be responsible for communicating needed information to the appropriate groups. The level of detail of the information communicated internally will probably be different from what is communicated to clients, board members, or other external stakeholders.

Clients may be focused on when a key milestone is reached to require training for their teams. Executives usually focus attention on problem areas and corrective actions and spend far less time wanting to know why a project is on schedule.

The senior leadership team is responsible for ensuring the various groups who need to be informed are identified, along with the level of information expected and the frequency of disseminating the information. This is documented in a Communications Plan developed by the person(s) responsible for communications.

Communication is key for establishing and maintaining organizational alignment to minimize surprises. The information being communicated should be clear, concise, and factual. Remember that people make up their own stories when they don't have all the facts. Communicate through multiple channels such as intranets, town halls, web meetings, and videos. Provide opportunities for questions to be presented and answered on a regular basis. When leading change initiatives, communicate the relevant information quickly to keep people informed. If there may be changes later, spell it out. Waiting until the last decision has been made or providing old information can be disastrous when leading change initiatives—eroding trust and credibility.

Communicating progress and celebrating early wins go a long way in building momentum. Of course, this assumes progress is being made, and there are wins to celebrate. You did set realistic deadlines upfront so there could be some wins, right?

Reflection Questions:

1. Have I assigned the area of communications to someone who has the skills, experience, and characteristics to perform the work?
2. Do I have an approved Communications Plan that outlines all the stakeholder groups and the frequency and type of information to be communicated?
3. Have I agreed on channels to be used to disseminate information on a regular basis?

CHAPTER 24

PROGRAM AUDITS AND REVIEWS

From time to time, it may be a good idea to complete an independent audit of the program to ensure a non-biased view of program or project management, financial management, and technical aspects.

If the initiative is a high-profile one and isn't going well, the board of directors or other outside entities will *help* by requesting audits of everything.

On one program of this nature (high profile and in the ditch), the board requested several audits, with one to two going on at any given time. Answering auditor questions during the day left the project teams little time to do the real work during normal business hours.

Don't assume all is well as an executive; it will be important to have unbiased reviews if there are concerns about the health of the initiative.

Obtaining this level of information early, along with root causes of problems, provides a better chance of taking corrective actions early, while it is easier to do so.

Experience shows once an executive is concerned about whether a program is on track or not, it's usually not, and it's usually worse than expected.

More times than not, there are multiple factors causing the issues: wrong people in the roles, poor understanding of requirements, unrealistic estimates, lack of communication, little or no accountability, not following the process, and the list continues. By the time a program or project heads south, there are several factors contributing to it. Getting insight into these areas early on provides the best chance of recovery.

In the general aviation world, there's almost never one mistake that caused an accident; rather, a series of poor judgments prevail. Decisions made might include: flying when tired or when you don't feel well (maybe you've taken some cold medicine), being in a hurry and not checking the weather quite as thoroughly as you should have, becoming distracted in the cockpit because you can't remember if you checked the oil or not, or you remembered too late you forgot to sump the fuel tanks to remove the water that may have condensed while the plane was sitting.

It's the same with managing any large-scale transformation program; it's hardly ever one solitary event that caused it to go sideways.

One of the reasons for this book is to ensure you, the executive, have a comprehensive understanding of the many dimensions to be considered for the successful delivery of change initiatives.

Reflection Questions:

1. Have there been audits or reviews of the projects comprising the change initiative?
2. What corrective actions were recommended resulting from the reviews? Have they been implemented?

OPERATIONAL READINESS

*"By failing to prepare, you are preparing
to fail."* ~ Benjamin Franklin

CHAPTER 25

PREPARING FOR GO-LIVE

P reparing to be operationally ready is an area sometimes minimized or started too late in the process. If systems are being implemented as part of the initiative, much of the focus is on the activities required for the specific part of the project, thinking once acceptance testing has been successfully completed, the bulk of the work has been done.

While system implementation is certainly a large part of the effort, it's usually about half the effort required to ready the staff for operationalizing it.

Sometimes the organizational structure of a company changes because of a large initiative to better align the reporting structure to a new way of doing business. In this case, the roles, responsibilities, and reporting structures need to be clearly defined and communicated before they can be put into place.

Ensuring operational readiness should be run like a project and planned for early in the project lifecycle, during the planning activities. During this time, the skills needed to

144 • JANET PLY, PHD

support the new environment can be assessed to determine if existing resources can be trained or if new ones need to be hired. Training programs are put into motion during this time as well. Assign someone to this project who has proven expertise in developing training programs for the scale and magnitude of your initiative.

Remember, availability is not a skill and this is a critical area for adoption—not a time to wing it. When possible, conduct a pilot with a group of friendly, early adopters who can help provide a forum for making course corrections and working out nuances otherwise overlooked or not readily visible during planning to move into the operations phase of the program.

TRAINING

Training can be quite a large undertaking and one often not given the attention needed.

It's not about teaching people how to use a system, but how to do their work from start to finish. Sometimes their work involves using other systems or following documented processes or procedures outside the systems.

One-way training telling someone how to do their job will not be sufficient. Assign resources who understand the concepts of adult learning and can take the required content and develop the appropriate learning.

The training environment should simulate the new way to work. This enables the people who will be doing the work time to practice with different scenarios until they feel comfortable. Track the training completed and provide knowledge assessments to ensure the participants can truly do the work. Allow sufficient time for people to be trained—this shouldn't be something they do in their spare time working it in when they can.

Schedule dedicated training time. Ensure the participants are focused, are provided an opportunity to ask questions, and become proficient. How well you do this will determine how well the new way of working is embraced and how quickly the business value will be recognized.

A formal Training Plan is recommended. This document includes:

- The target audience(s) requiring training (external sources may also require training)
- How the training will be conducted (online, in-person, video, web meeting)
- How training effectiveness will be measured (knowledge assessments)
- Training required for each role
- Requirements for the training environment
- How completed training will be tracked for each person.

Setting up a training environment can be time-consuming, especially when data needs to be synchronized to simulate different data states along the way, or there are handoffs to different roles.

These scenarios need to be thoroughly tested before training starts. If you try to train people when the environment has not been thoroughly vetted, you undermine the confidence of the participants. Rumors spread about how money has been wasted on something that isn't going to work.

Gaining the adoption you need from your staff is hard enough when all goes well. Don't provide opportunities for complaining because of a lack of planning.

KNOWLEDGE TRANSFER

If consultants are working on the program, schedule time for knowledge transfer to the appropriate people who will be taking over the consultants' work.

Like training, knowledge transfer needs to be a well-defined workstream to ensure the knowledge has indeed been transferred to staff members, and they are comfortable taking ownership of the work. Some consulting firms aren't eager to transfer their knowledge to your staff since they lose billable revenue when they are no longer performing the work. In several of my client experiences, there were no deliverables for knowledge transfer, and consultants were kept on long after they were needed.

Make knowledge transfer a deliverable in the contract with consulting firms to provide an incentive for this to be a priority. Start this activity early in the project versus waiting until the last minute.

Knowledge transfer isn't just intended for consultants who are leaving the project. It also pertains to employees who may be taking on new assignments and training their successors. Identify candidates who will be taking over the work assignments and provide sufficient overlap with the departing individual to learn and understand the role.

USER SUPPORT

Providing steller user support, once the systems or changes go live, is critical to accelerate adoption and minimize frustrations.

Adequately staff the Help Desk and adequtely train each member of the team. Be prepared to answer lots of questions in the beginning. Provide sufficient and trained staff, especially in the beginning, to minimize user wait times.

Assign super users across the organization who are well prepared to help train and provide support as needed. These are usually the SMEs assigned to help define the future state processes, work on defining the requirements, participate in user acceptance testing, and likely training. By the time they have finished this level of involvement, they are well prepared to assist others in learning the new way of doing business. (You DID assign your best SMEs to do the work described, didn't you? Good, I thought so.)

Knowing who to contact should be readily available whenever there are questions—and there will be a lot in the beginning.

USER ACCESS

If software solutions are a component of the change initiative, establishing the proper user access is important to ensure people can do their work.

Know who the users are, the types of access needed by role, which role each person should be assigned to, and set up user accounts and passwords. This shouldn't be a difficult area to get right if properly planned out. The frustration caused by not having the correct access to do your job contributes to the lack of adoption and the attitude of, "things don't work." When rolling out the time-tracking system described above (remember the slacker tracker?), there were a few early resistors who didn't have access to all the areas needed in the system. They used this as a reason why they didn't want to use it and it didn't work. Take the time needed to set this up correctly, and it will reduce the number of calls to the Help Desk as well as user frustration.

Data Sources and Quality

Don't underestimate the impact data has on a change initiative when data sources change or years of data need to be migrated into new system repositories. Routinely, this area turns out to be more complex than expected and takes much longer to convert than planned for—sometimes becoming the critical path.

Software vendors are notorious for giving implementation schedules based on just the software piece. Somewhere in the fine print of the agreement with the vendor is mention of something like:

> *"The customer has responsibility for ensuring that their data is complete and accurate and can be imported with the push of a button."*

Data cleanup is almost always more complex and time-consuming than expected. One of my financial clients had grown primarily through acquisitions, having acquired more than 400 companies. This client had an initiative to move from a decentralized holding company model to a centralized operating company, standardizing its business processes and systems across all the acquired companies. Most of the effort expended on this project was data cleanup and standardization.

There are several common problems to consider when data migration is involved:

1. **Disparate data repositories.** Every company accumulates data, and most likely, it's housed in

multiple databases or repositories. Knowing where all the data is housed is the first step in figuring out the complexity of the migration.

2. **Quality of the source data.** Often, there is missing data, duplicate data, fields with misspellings. Cleaning this up in advance takes time and can be started early in the process.

3. **Understanding the data.** While some fields are straightforward, there are many times when custom fields are used to house data that doesn't fit anywhere else or when additional fields are needed. Custom fields may not be well documented, may change over time, or may not be used uniformly. Being aware of these types of fields saves time downstream when migrating and testing the data.

4. **Multiple sources of data.** It's not uncommon for organizations to use different tools. Some locations may use spreadsheets; others may use different vendor technologies. Seldom do spreadsheet users document data fields and definitions, leading to errors and challenging data transformations.

5. **Data specifications.** With multiple data sources, and with some being old and no longer supported, it can be difficult to understand what each field means. Figuring this out in advance of the migration saves time and a lot of headaches later.

6. **Data testing.** Simply migrating the data is not enough—it must be validated by testing. Sufficient test cases to validate the data are essential to ensure the data migrated yields the expected results.

7. **Collaboration on Data.** While there may be experts in data migration, users of the data should be consulted as they are probably the ones who defined which custom fields to use and why. Business users can assist in developing data test cases and testing the data migration. Business users of the data should be part of the data migration team and brought in early.

8. **Data security.** Migrating data from one (or more) platforms comes with risks. It could be leaked or accessed by unauthorized users. Having security controls in place for the migration efforts could save the company the pain coming from having a data breach and the loss of credibility when the breach makes its way to headlines seen around the world.

READINESS ASSESSMENT

Prior to going live, especially when software solutions are involved, put a formal check in place to catch issues.

A few items to consider when conducting a readiness assessment are:

- Environments are properly set up and configured.
- Testing scenarios are comprehensive and successfully passed.
- User accounts are ready with appropriate levels of access.
- Necessary training has been conducted.
- Team members are ready to perform the work.
- Team members know who to contact for help.
- Team members know where to find processes and procedures.
- Super Users are in place and available.

- Help Desk staff have been trained and are prepared to answer questions.
- Data conversions are complete.
- Compliance and regulatory requirements are properly addressed.
- Appropriate levels of security are in place..

The scope of a readiness assessment is dependent on several factors: how changes are being rolled out (e.g., incrementally or flip the switch), the number of people impacted, the complexity of the changes, security requirements, compliance, regulatory requirements, the number of locations, and such.

Adjust the scope of the readiness assessment appropriately.

Reflection Questions:

1. Is there a project to ensure the organization is operationally prepared to implement and function with the changes brought about by the change initiative?
2. Has sufficient end-to-end testing been completed to provide a level of confidence in moving changes into production?
3. Have consultants completed a knowledge transfer to your staff for their work?

PROJECT CLOSEOUT

"Great is the art of beginning,
but greater the art is of ending."
~Henry Wadsworth Longfellow

CHAPTER 26

ALL DONE

A s projects are completed, it's important to close out each one. You *will* know when the project is finished, right?

It's not uncommon to have projects linger and resources continue to charge time to them. As soon as the project is complete, finalize any charges such as time or materials, and close the account codes to avoid additional expenses being incurred.

Sometimes team members lose focus as project completion nears. It's a part of the *humans are messy* statement earlier. There may be concerns as to their next assignment and whether there will be one. If losing the talent would jeopardize the work, there may be a need for retention bonuses for key personnel, tied to performance and completion of the work.

All project deliverables should be signed off and approved before the project is marked complete. Archive all the project documentation in a repository where it can be easily retrieved, including close-out documentation. This is usually the responsibility of the PMO.

Oftentimes, once a project is completed, the results are transitioned to a new team for implementation or use. Be sure this transition is complete, and the information required is available. Just throwing it over the wall to the next team is a bad idea.

Conduct a Lessons Learned meeting at the end of each project to determine what went well and what could be changed for improvement. The Lessons Learned meetings can be held early in the project's life cycle as well to enable course corrections to be made. At a minimum, hold one at the end of the project for continuous improvement opportunities and communicate the findings to the appropriate people.

Once the closeout work has been completed, the remaining staff can be reassigned. Contractors can be released or reassigned to help on other projects.

Reflection Questions:

1. Is there a clear definition of what done means for each workstream?
2. Have Lessons Learned been documented and communicated for use on other projects?

CHAPTER 27

SUMMARY

C hange initiatives are complex, requiring
exceptional leadership to orchestrate the myriad
of projects and tasks that must be completed
across multiple functional areas.

The first section, *Readiness—You, Your Team, and Your
Organization*, provided a description of what it means to
manage change: being aware of organizational readiness for
change, understanding the why and vision of the change,
organizational alignment, the human aspects of change
management, executive sponsorship, and the right team.

The second section, *Art—Leading People Through Change*
covered topics on leadership, learning from others, and
building teams and relationships. The section on *Science—
Building a Powerful Project Plan* provided information on
tactical aspects of portfolio management, team organization,
putting systems in place, knowing who the stakeholders are,
financial aspects, and the need and use of various support
organizations.

We covered the aspects of implementation, including topics on how to kick off the initiative, using external resources, establishing a Program Management Office (PMO), and Planning.

The *Sustainability—Manage, Measure, and Adjust* section covered monitoring progress, managing scope communications, and the needs for audits and reviews.

The section on *Operational Readiness* covered training, knowledge transfer, user support and access, data sources and quality, and conducting a readiness assessment to ensure all systems are a go.

Lastly comes *Project Closeout* where we discussed the needed work to be performed as projects are completed.

There is a saying, *"No plan survives first contact with the enemy."* This certainly applies to change initiatives.

No matter how prepared you think you are for moving forward with changes, it rarely goes according to plan. Expect to roll with the flow and pivot as information is gained, then course-correct along the way.

It is my sincere hope you benefit from the experiences and knowledge gained during the journey of my consulting career, and this book contributes to making your change initiatives part of the successful 30 percent!

ACKNOWLEDGMENTS

I have been fortunate to have a successful consulting career spanning over 25+ years and many clients across multiple industries. Thank you to each client for allowing me to be a part of your change initiative journeys. The experiences gained in each engagement provided professional and personal growth I could never have imagined (or learned in school!). Not to mention, the engagements served as great examples and lessons learned throughout the book.

A very special thank you to Pete Hoelscher, who played a key role in organizing the content, suggested the use of reflection questions, and added humor, as only Pete can do!

Thank you to Tammi Terry, Bob Williamson, Dr. Stan Rifkin, and Janet Eden-Harris for your reviews, insightful comments, and encouragement!

All of you have made this book and me better!

APPENDIX–SUMMARY OF REFLECTION QUESTIONS

1. Do I have a good understanding of the magnitude of the impact of the change initiative?
2. Have I selected a change management approach for leading the change aspects of the initiative?
3. Do I have a good understanding of the scope of the initiative?
4. Should an organizational readiness assessment be conducted?
5. Have I aligned compensation, recognition, and reinforcement to support the organizational change?
6. What steps have I taken to put individual and team goals, at all levels, in sync with the company goals?
7. Is the vision communicated in terms appropriate to all levels within the company?
8. Do I have someone on staff who has the characteristics to be an effective executive sponsor (if it's not me)? If not, how will I find and incent the person?
9. Am I prepared to provide constant and visible support to this person to increase the odds of success?
10. Is the executive sponsor taking on a pass or fail assignment? Why or why not?
11. If using a consulting company, do I have a clear understanding of what work should be completed by them and what I must be responsible for?

12. Does the leadership team understand how the change initiative fits into the overall organizational strategy?

13. Does each leader have clarity around his or her role?

14. Do I have measurement and reporting in place evaluate and track the effectiveness of the project?

15. Is there clarity around who the decision-makers are and how decisions will be made?

16. Have I completed an assessment of the leadership team to determine if each person has the right skills and experience to lead his or her area?

17. Do the leaders have the right attributes for leading a change initiative?

18. Do I have the right people on the bus?

19. Does the leadership team possess the desired leadership characteristics and experience to successfully lead the change initiative, including trust, credibility, and influence?

20. Do I have a good understanding of the concerns and fears of the people who will be affected by the change and a plan in place to manage this?

21. Who do I know I can speak with who has experience in leading change initiatives ?

22. Am I (and my leadership team) willing to listen and learn from others?

23. Successful change is contingent upon several key factors or drivers. Do I know the drivers of my change? If so, how will I locate other learners who faced the same or similar drivers?

24. What are the characteristics of my team? Do these characteristics point to high performance or dysfunctionality?

25. Are team-building activities scheduled regularly?

26. How am I as a leader, along with my leadership team, intentionally building rapport with my teams?

27. Does the organization have a clear understanding of what constitutes projects and programs?

28. Is there an effective portfolio management practice in place?

29. Are the project workloads aligned with the available resources and budget?

30. Is there governance in place to ensure alignment of work efforts across the organization?

31. Has the initiative's organization structure been developed with clearly defined projects and support areas?

32. Are the roles and responsibilities clearly defined and communicated?

33. Do project team members understand the reporting structure?

34. Are we taking the necessary time to ensure we are putting practices in place to position the change initiative to be successful?

35. Are we working on processes for the sake of doing something instead of ensuring it's the right task?

36. Have projects had to be redone where the rework could've been prevented had proper time been taken?

37. Do I know who the stakeholders are and their interests?

38. What is the plan in place for managing stakeholder requests?

39. Am I using an effective medium for keeping stakeholders informed?

40. Is there a defined approach for how to manage the financials of the change initiative?

41. Are the right controls and reporting in place for tracking the financials?

42. Is there a way to determine if the costs incurred are appropriate for work performed?

43. Do I have representatives from Compliance on the teams to provide requirements?

44. Is my HR leader engaged and capable of providing the staffing needs, support for change management, and needed communications?

45. Have my contracts been thoughtfully developed and executed by those who have the requisite skills?

46. Is my training leader engaged and capable of providing the training needed?

47. Are my finance and project teams working closely together to provide insights on budget and schedule performance?

48. Have I prepared well for the kickoff meeting(s) required to align the teams with the work to be performed?

49. Does everyone understand their individual and team roles?

50. Were clear and realistic expectations set during the kickoff meeting?

51. Do I have a clear understanding of why a vendor is needed and the services they will provide?

52. How will I manage vendor performance?

53. What happens if a vendor fails to perform in accordance with their contract?

54. Was the vendor contract structured with the proper legal support?

55. Is a PMO setup to effectively manage and report on the change initiative?

56. Does the PMO provide reporting showing the information needed for decision-making?

57. What are the PMO tracking, reporting, and mitigating risks and issues?

58. Is the PMO proactive in escalating issues needing executive attention?

59. Have the current and future state business processes been mapped out?

60. Have the proper resources gathered requirements in a way understood by the appropriate teams?

61. Is the overall schedule based on the requirements?

62. Are the tasks documented and linked to provide a high-level schedule for the initiative?

63. Do I have the right people for the work they are assigned?

64. Has the workload of the key team members been adjusted to allow for the time needed to support this initiative?

65. Have I backfilled key positions where team members are required full time on the initiative?

66. Do I have enough status information to determine how the change initiative work is progressing, where there are problem areas, and where executive attention is required?

67. Are there regularly scheduled meetings with the senior leadership team for reviews?

68. Are project audits or reviews scheduled to ensure the accuracy of the processes and information presented?

69. Are there baselined requirements changes can be submitted against?

70. Is an effective Change Control Board in place for managing change requests?

71. Are there defined criteria for deciding when a change is approved or rejected?

72. Have I assigned the area of communications to someone who has the skills, experience, and characteristics to perform the work?

73. Do I have an approved Communications Plan outlining all the stakeholder groups and the frequency and type of information to be communicated?

74. Is there a project to ensure the organization is operationally prepared to implement and function with the changes brought about by the change initiative?

75. Has sufficient end-to-end testing been completed to provide a level of confidence in moving changes into production?

76. Have consultants completed a knowledge transfer to your staff for their work?

77. Is there a clear definition of what completed means for each workstream?

78. Have Lessons Learned been documented and communicated for use on other projects?

ABOUT THE AUTHOR

Janet Ply, PhD

Janet has a passion for helping leaders and companies be successful. She has over 25 years' experience in leading transformation initiatives and leadership development – serving companies across multiple industries ranging in size from startup to Fortune 50.

Janet works with the C-Suite of organizations to build leadership competencies. She provides practical training, coaching, and mentoring in leadership and program management, transferring her knowledge and experience to client teams.

She holds a PhD in Information Technology from George Mason University, an MS in Engineering from UT Austin, an MS in Procurement and Acquisition, and a BS in Mathematics. She has been a guest lecturer at the Texas McCombs Graduate School of Business and an adjunct professor in a Master's program in Project Management and is a frequent speaker on topics related to leadership, managing change initiatives, program management, and process improvement.

Janet is an instrument-rated pilot and enjoys flying Angel Flight missions for patients who need transportation to and from medical treatment.

Made in the USA
Monee, IL
15 October 2021

80070840R00098